VENTURA:

Mystic City
by the Sea

Mystically yours, Maurine Moore

Maurine Moore

⭐ Seaview Publishing

VENTURA: Mystic City by the Sea

Copyright © 2000 Maurine Moore
P.O. Box 2195, Ventura, CA 93002-2195
Phone: 805/643-7650
E-mail: maurinee@juno.com

☆ Seaview Publishing
P.O. Box 2625, Ventura, CA 93002-2625

Cover design by Margaret Macknelly

Book design by Mary Embree

ISBN 0-9700682-1-2

Printed in the United States of America

Acknowledgments

Richard Senate, local historian and ghost expert, has been so generous with his time and expertise, a simple acknowledgment cannot possibly express my gratitude. Without his input this book would be half as long and not nearly as interesting. He allowed me to quote extensively from the booklet, *Ventura: Tidbits and Trivia.* His *Erle Stanley Gardner's Ventura: The Birthplace of Perry Mason* is the prevailing source of information about the world's most popular mystery writer.

Along with friends, acquaintances, bookstore owners and any one else who showed an interest, Richard helped me select the title. Originally titled *Ventura's Nooks and Crannies,* we decided *Ventura: Mystic City by the Sea* would describe the contents more accurately and appeal to a wider readership.

Charles Johnson, busy librarian at the Ventura County Museum of History & Art, shared his extensive knowledge about stories surrounding the haunted Nye Mansion and other sites of interest in San Buenaventura.

Thanks to Dave Mason, Ojai historian, for stories about the railroad between Ojai and Ventura and the fascinating tale of Amelda's Guest Ranch.

Bridge buddies, JoAnn Bowen, Polly Wassell, Marilyn Brett, and Jan Steele gave me ideas and articles and occasionally accompanied me to places I was reluctant to go alone. Jan and her husband, Gene, deserve special thanks for proofreading the book and making positive comments and suggestions. Mary Dodd proofread and edited the book. They all offered many suggestions that were worthwhile and made it much more interesting.

Whenever I entangled a female companion in an escapade which caused discomfort I preserved her anonymity by referring to her as "Ami," which means friend.

Another friend, Mary Embree, a professional editor and writer, offered encouragement and excellent suggestions and took on the formidable task of typesetting and helping me get the book published.

Daughters Vivian and Jill have stood by me in this endeavor as they have stood by me throughout their lives, careful to offer constructive advice instead of criticism. They both helped me learn how to use my new computer. My daughter Jill's colleague from England, Margaret Macknelly, designed this book's cover and also created the map of Ventura which appears in it.

The old city of San Buenaventura must be included for if she had not cast her spell upon me I never would have taken the time to become better acquainted.

Introduction

San Buenaventura, the "Good Fortune" city, was named after a Franciscan monk who acquired it in an unusual manner. As a child he was once taken so seriously ill he was not expected to live. His distraught parents took him to Saint Francis of Assisi hoping for a miracle. The Fray prayed over the child and, to everyone's astonishment, he recovered. Upon learning of this cure Saint Francis exclaimed, "What good fortune!" After the youngster grew up and became a monk he took Buenaventura as his spiritual name.

This mystic city by the sea has a colorful history. Battles, murders, mysteries, intrigues, infidelities, tragedies and tales of great courage emerge as the mist rolls away and we delve into the stories that lie hidden.

Mitc-ka-na-kan natives, later called Chumash, were the region's first inhabitants. San Buenaventura and all of California became part of Mexico when that country won its independence from Spain in 1822. After the United States victory in the Mexican War in 1848, California became a U. S. territory—just in time for the Gold Rush of 1849, when Anglo men and women settled in the area in increasing numbers.

Spirits hovering about remind us there are secrets that have gone before we may never know, just as there are forces securely hidden from view. Revealing them could unleash another spirit, another misadventure that those who do not believe in the supernatural would find unsettling.

Not all the people, places and things you will read about here are mysterious; some are as familiar as the Von's Deli or a neighbor's yard filled with roses. And, just as Alice found when she went through the looking glass, some encounters are unexpected.

I am reminded of a conversation with a fellow author at a Western Writer's of America (WWA) convention some years ago when he was talking about the small city where he lived.

The main industry of this area was raising chickens. Many trucks carrying the fowl passed along the city streets, strewing white feathers. As a result, the gutters were eternally lined with fluffy stuff that looked like snow. This is not something their Chamber of Commerce would have told anyone who asked for information.

Many of the stories you find within these pages are not what our Chamber of Commerce would tell you, either. The street people, the scandals, the nude beach are the underbelly of our community, not the image Ventura's promoters would want visitors to have. Yet all of these facets are part of the fabric of our local society, and for this reason have been included.

Most of the ghosts I have encountered in San Buenaventura are protective spirits, not those bent upon vengeance. But do not be surprised as you wander about this paradise if, at some unexpected time, you turn a corner or glance over your shoulder and find yourself in the presence of an apparition with a tale of woe or haunting story it desperately needs to tell.

Foreword

My sojourn to this place I had never heard of began in 1988 when the children left home to live their own lives and a seventeen-year love affair ended. That was when I departed Cheyenne, Wyoming, to seek a warmer clime.

For decades I lived in Colorado, Wyoming and Utah. Once I was free to go anywhere, like the Pisces I am, I was inevitably drawn to the ocean's shores.

If you have ever had the experience, after searching for years, of finding something that fit perfectly and was exactly what you wanted, you will know how I felt when I found Ventura. This is the place where I hope to spend the rest of my life . . . this is home.

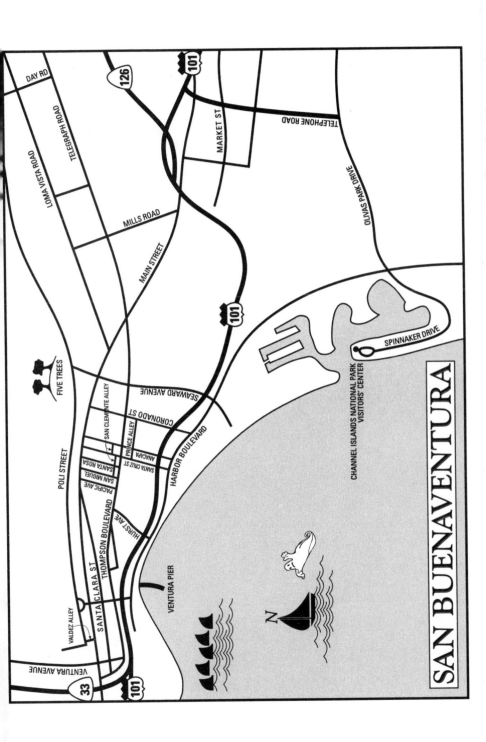

SAN BUENAVENTURA

CONTENTS

VENTURA:

Mystic City by the Sea

CHAPTER ONE

VENTURA AVENUE

A mist shrouds the city and in the distance a foghorn warns of treacherous, rock-strewn shoals. It has been this way all night, a welcome sound for those who love the sea.

Like ocean ports the world over, Ventura has a haunted legacy. Legends abound and spirits wander through old buildings, cemeteries and parks. Most of these apparitions are kind; a few are mischievous.

As this adventure begins, you (the reader) and I, drift like the fog, engulfing a few of the people, places and things in town, stopping briefly at others, skipping some altogether. Though most of these have attracted me because of the good energy they radiate, I discovered darker spirits. Skulking, they wait their turn. Too powerful to be ignored forever, they appear at unexpected times to remind us that what appears on the surface is not always what lies hidden below.

As the sun warms the air, the marine layer gracefully retreats and the city emerges.

San Buenaventura's birth was spawned by the discovery of gold at Sutter's Mill in 1848. After the gold rush many people drifted southward and settled near the missions founded by the monks in the 18th Century.

On January 23, 1925, oil was discovered in the Ventura Avenue Field. Lloyd #6 came in with 5,460 barrels of crude per day, one of the richest in the state. The oil boom changed the town, causing the population to triple in the next five years. Driving along the 33 freeway to Ojai, many of the pumps are still visible, still pulling the dark liquid from the earth.

The mist lingers heavily along the banks of the Ventura River. It is here the city began and here our journey commences with one of the newest and most inviting recreational sites in the area, The Ventura River Trail.

The Bike Path

This charming trail, connecting Ventura with Ojai, once called Nordhoff, has a colorful history.

> Puff, puff, chug, chug, went the little blue engine. I think I can, I think I can, I think I can, I think I can, I think I can, I think I can. Up, up, up. Faster and faster and faster the little engine climbed until at last it reached the top of the mountain. Down in the valley lay the city.
>
> —From *The Little Engine that Could,* Watty Piper, 1930

Residents of Nordhoff, hoping to attract a "better class of people" than those who came by way of the hazardous 12-hour stage ride, began their campaign for a rail line to connect them with San Buenaventura in the middle of the 19th century. It was not until 1898, however, that they were successful.

The construction commenced in 1897 with the help of 95 mules. The workers didn't waste time as the animals could eat up the profits.

The railroad track was officially abandoned in December 1969 after a series of washouts, but the remaining sections continued to mar the landscape until 1980. At this time the County of Ventura acquired the land from the Southern Pacific and eventually built a horse and bike trail on the narrow stretch. Today horses, hikers and bicyclists make excellent use of this century old scenic pathway.

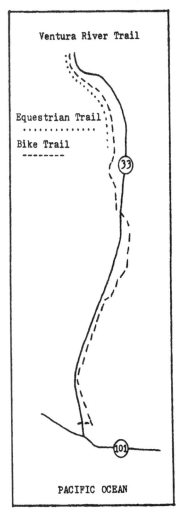

Trail improvements include a 12-foot-wide paved bicycle path and an adjacent 6-foot-wide unpaved walking path for the entire length. A 12-foot-wide equestrian trail, approximately three-quarters of a mile long and ending at the northern edge of the Canada Larga Channel, is also included.

Amenities along the trail include a variety of wood and chain link fencing, intermittent landscaping, trail signage, directional, safety and interpretive panels, and several displays of public art.

Repeated inquiries about the artworks scheduled have met with little success. A muralist gave me the name of someone who has been commissioned to paint a mural "somewhere." A sculptor said he was making a windmill. Another person said certain areas had been given to artisans to do whatever they wanted. When their creations are finished it will be interesting to see what everyone has done—and what the forces that play tricks on us have undone.

The *California Vehicle Code* was created to protect the safety of pedestrians and cyclists. It is filled with important information. Here is an example.

> 🚲 Passengers must have a separate seat and passengers under four years of age or 40 pounds must have protection from moving parts, and must wear a helmet.

A memory wafts back to a time I was giving my four-year-old daughter a ride on the handlebars of a bicycle and her foot got caught in the spokes. We flipped over and landed upright on the pavement, not severely hurt. We were lucky no cars were around; unlucky so many neighbors were watching.

Recent History

The Ventura River Trail was partially washed out in the floods that caused the Ventura River to overflow its banks a few years ago. It begins east of the Ventura Pier, curves north when it arrives at the river and parallels the "Avenue," which is what locals call Ventura Avenue. The trail is full of surprises, not all of them pleasant.

Scattered about are abandoned grocery carts used by homeless people as mobile dwellings. They gleam on the river banks, a testament to those who quietly inhabit the area at night. With the trail nearly complete, the carts may have disappeared, along with a fair number of other things mentioned in this book when I began writing it.

One story an Avenue landlord recounts is of a man who lived beneath a tree until the raging waters destroyed his "home." As a result, he claimed he qualified for aid, and the officials concurred. They installed him in a one-bedroom apartment that cost taxpayers $650 per month.

When the trail is finished it will be an easily followed path that runs for several miles through Casitas Springs and Foster Park, and bicycling enthusiasts can enjoy a scenic, safe ride all the way to Ojai.

The Fix-it Shop

The first stop after leaving the bike trail is the fix-it shop at 1540 North Ventura Avenue. Upon entering you notice the good energy at once. The owner, Huey Young, takes pride in the work he does, and charges a fair price. "It won't break again," he promised after I had a lamp repaired several years ago. And it never has. If you are searching for a repairman who does a good job, try Huey's place.

Players Card Club

The card club, 906 North Ventura Avenue, offers residents and guests the opportunity to play poker from 10 a.m. to 2 a.m. every day. They play Hold Em, Omaha, Pineapple and Lo-Ball with no limit on Hold Em on Wednesday and Saturday.

The club is open to the public and offers food service. A big "Ladies Welcome" sign invites members of that gender to participate. A mid-morning visit on a weekday, however, finds a large room crowded with tables and players but not a woman in sight.

I got mixed feelings about this place, perhaps because I've had bad experiences with a gambler. And, though the reception was cordial and the ambiance friendly, it's really dark inside, even on the sunniest of days.

But since people seemed to be having a good time and the manager assured me anyone wishing to play is welcome, the weird feeling may derive from my overactive imagination.

Avenue Tire and Service

Gene Plueger's tire operation, 617 North Ventura Avenue, offers 24-hour road service and a lot of friendly advice. Purchase tires here and the staff will take care of them for you until you need new ones. Though it is not a traditional garage, brake and front end alignment services have recently been added.

The charm of this place is not in the type or quality of work they do, but in the personality of its owner. Plueger has been a resident of Ventura since the middle of the century. He knows everyone in town, and everyone in town, especially along the Avenue, knows Gene. The fact those who know him invariably speak well of the man is a testament to his commitment to helping people—especially women who may desperately need it, or at least need information about a place where they can get their vehicle problems solved, or a plumber who is reliable and offers reasonable rates. Are you moving? He knows people who will lift and carry, are honest, and happy to help you out. He has also opened a halfway house for young men who are struggling to stay clean of drugs and alcohol. Anyone exploring Ventura Avenue will do well to make his acquaintance. Guys like Gene are difficult to find.

The Mural at Simpson and Ventura Avenue

Cattycornered across the street from Avenue Tire is a mural with a highly controversial history. It was commissioned with the aid of government monies as a project for "at risk" kids.

Aided by muralist M. B. Hanrahan, the young people created a rather lurid "Don't Do Drugs" motif with needles and blood that drove home a strong message. The original owner sold the building to a man who installed a liquor store in it. The new owner was picking up such negative vibes from the mural he painted over it!

A couple of lawsuits ensued with the artist and kids winning both. So now, though the needles and blood are gone, the mural is back.

Avenue Hardware, Inc.

This hardware store at 481 North Ventura Avenue is a vanishing phenomenon. With competition from the huge discount outlets, this family owned and operated business thrives on individualized service and a large selection of products. Plumbing and electrical supplies, cutlery, hand and power tools and Rustoleum paints are examples of the inventory carried on its shelves.

Currently owned by Tad Dewire, the store opened in 1927 and was purchased on a handshake in 1943 from the Harvey family. Apparent the moment you enter the store is the strong pride the employees radiate in the products and services this organization offers. Those who need professional advice and appreciate personal attention will like Avenue Hardware. I often go out of my way to do business with them.

The House on Memory Lane

For viewing only, a residence on the Avenue evokes childhood memories. One of my mother Helen O'Dell's best friends, Joyce Carrico, lived in such a place, across the street from the public library in my hometown, Lamar, Colorado.

Both houses have a front porch and a porte-cochere at the side. The sheltering entry protects visitors from the rain, wind, and snow.

This old house in Lamar was the scene of one of my first spooky experiences. Visiting the Carrico's daughter, Judy, she led me down into their dark basement and told me stories of evil things that had happened there. Though I was only six or seven and vulnerable because my older siblings, Jane and Bob, were always scaring me, I remember how incongruous this seemed. Judy's mother was down there doing laundry and she didn't seem frightened, so why should I be?

Whether that dark basement was haunted or not I don't know. Whenever I return, people seem reluctant to talk about it.

The Old Library

The home on the Avenue brings back pleasant memories of trips to the library in Lamar. Built in the center of the block, you reached it by walking along tree-shaded sidewalks that radiated out from the building to the corners. The entrance faced directly across the street to the Carrico's front porch.

Porches have disappeared from homes now, the space being incorporated into the living areas. The library in Lamar is gone, too, giving way to the inevitable. One building on an entire city block seemed a big waste of space and too attractive a location for the city's officials to leave it alone.

I understand from folks at home the Carrico's place is still there. I am reminded of it every time I drive along the Avenue.

Hell's Angels

Located on Fix Way, a block long thoroughfare between Ventura Avenue and Garden Street, you will find the international headquarters of this organization with the fearsome reputation. Casual inquiries around the city uncover some interesting information. At the time of my visit they were in trouble with the police. This trouble was not for illegal drugs or other matters which should concern the police, a member claimed, but had something to do with paying taxes. Since his explanation doesn't make much sense, it is left to the imagination what the problem really is as the cops who were asked plead ignorance.

Rumors, rumors. You have to have killed someone in order to join, is one of them. Some years ago an article in a women's magazine described sordid sexual rites the Angels performed with their women. Are these things true?

An aspiring initiate was reluctant to give me any information, though I swore I had no ulterior motives for asking. He did admit a man named George Christi was the head of the organization, and you had to have a motorcycle and be able to ride well before you could become a full-fledged member, but he told me nothing else.

In an attempt to verify some of the stories, I approached the bright red metal barriers at the front of the headquarters building on Fix Way, wondering whether they were barred to keep people in or to keep people out.

The gates were securely locked and no doorbell or buzzer was in sight. The inner door was open, and though it was so dark inside I couldn't see anything, I could hear someone talking, so I said, "Hello?" The bad vibes I picked up were reinforced by what happened next.

"Whadda ya want?"
"May I come in?"
"No!"
"Is George Christi here?"
"He won't be here till later on this afternoon."
"May I talk to you?"
"I'm on the phone." In other words, get lost.
"Okay. I'll come back later."

One of the tales is not a rumor. Having lived in Cheyenne, Wyoming, for two decades, I was often involved with Frontier Days, a famous rodeo that attracts hundreds of thousands of visitors to that small western city every summer during the last week in July. Cheyennites, and especially members of The Frontier Days Committee, are proud of the fairgrounds, and the racetrack and grandstands. One summer some members of a motorcycle gang, rumored to be Hell's Angels, decided to have a little fun and started racing around the track on their bikes.

Most of the ranchers in Wyoming know how to handle a rope.

This is especially true of the ones who compete in roping events during Frontier Days. In a modern version of Frontier Justice the cowboys took serious exception to this travesty. They lassoed the bikers, dragged them to the city limits and told them to get out of town and stay out.

The Hell's Angels add a great deal of color to our community. I have never heard anyone object to their presence. Though the law enforcement community keeps a close watch over them, they seem law-abiding enough. Fearsome reputation and my own misgivings aside, I suspect they are just a bunch of bikers bent on having a good time.

Johnny's Mexican Food

At the corner of Ventura Avenue and Fix Way, we find Johnny's, one of Ventura's many Mexican restaurants.

"Sure we have printed menus you can take," a friendly gentleman said as he handed one through the service window. "What can I do for you?"

"Nothing right now, but I'll be back."

I glanced at the menu. Along the side it said, "Voted Best Burrito in Sunset Magazine, May '96. Eat in or take out. Open Tuesday through Saturday, 9 a.m. to 6 p.m."

"Order anything you want," I magnanimously offered my friend, JoAnn, a few days later when we went there for dinner.

"Yeah, right," she responded, ordering two tacos. "Oh, wait a minute," she said when she saw a sign that they were on sale for 50¢. "I thought tacos were fifty cents only on Saturdays."

"We made too many," the cheerful woman waiting on us explained, as behind her a young man immersed three taco shells in a pot of boiling oil.

Freshly made? Not already cooked and ready to be filled at a moment's notice? It took a little longer to get them, but who cared? The wait promised to be worth it.

"How do you know tacos are always fifty cents on Saturdays?" I asked JoAnn, a long-time Ventura resident. "Do you eat here often?"

"When the kids were little I did. This place was a labor of love for Johnny. They keep hours now, but he didn't. He opened early and stayed open late. He enjoyed visiting with people as much as he enjoyed feeding them."

"Your order's ready," the woman called.
"How much?"
"Four dollars and fifty cents. Would you like something to drink? We have milk or coffee."

We passed on the drinks and I suggested we go to my place. "I'll buy you a beer," I offered, feeling somewhat guilty about the small tab, a little better about the large tip I had left.

"Let's stay here," JoAnn said, biting happily into a taco. "And get some hot sauce."

It is not a fancy eatery. Tucked in near the end of Ventura Avenue across from the Von's Shopping Center, customers order while standing on the sidewalk. You can eat on paper plates in a side room furnished with picnic tables or take the food home.

The food was so good and the ambiance so pleasant it's no wonder Johnny's is a local treasure.

Meanwhile, let's walk across the Avenue to Von's and check out their deli, one of the best in town.

Von's Deli
The grocery store is at the corner of Ventura Avenue and Main

Street. Employees bustle about and customers throng the aisles even on weekdays, attracted by the pleasant ambiance and delightful delicatessen. A colorful brochure illustrates what is included with their party platters.

The Entertainer, The Lavosh Tray, Super Sub Sandwich, Spinach Dip Platter, The Deluxe and Tiny-But-Tasty.

Other menu items are

Fabulous Fruit Tray, Golden Crisp Medly, Jalapeno Artichoke Dip, Mini Croissants, The Salad Sampler and Chicken Snack and Let's Celebrate Tray, and Bean Dip, sold by the pound. *Thank You For Ordering Your Party Needs From Von's.*

We're now going to visit one of the most creative nooks in the state, perhaps in the world.

Art City

Peking Street, which nestles under the 33 Freeway, is three blocks west of Ventura Avenue. Scouting around for those doing art work on the River Trail, I came upon this short street with the Oriental name almost by accident.

How could I have lived in Ventura nearly a decade and never known about Art City? Though my interests lie elsewhere, this is a small town and many of my friends are members of the city's cultural community.

The first attraction is the name, Peking Avenue. Surely this was so designated when Chinatown, ousted from Figueroa Street, settled nearer the Ventura River.

Was this displacement of our early-day Chinese citizens why I was picking up such a strange feeling? It didn't make much sense, but the nebulous energy we get from spirits rarely does. I read some of the Art City literature it to see if it held any clues.

One of the brochures explains what the sculpture studios are all about:

> The studios at Art City are a composite of professional artists working in various mediums who share the facilities and each other's knowledge.

> Art City is intended to showcase both in-house and outside artists including sculpture, painting, and photography.

Continuous art shows are staged in the 2,000-square-foot Gallery and range from single artist to group showings, poetry readings, performance pieces and musical events.

The final result is Art City Sculpture, perfect for the artist, art enthusiast, and buyer to relax and enjoy these creations in a friendly environment.

Art City's services include consulting for designers and land-scape architects, carving seminars with hands-on weekend workshops presenting various techniques, and Pronto Tools for sculpture.

The studio has specimen carving stones available in alabaster, soapstone, marble, and onyx that have been chosen for integrity, shape, and color. They claim the assortment available is likely the best the sculptor will find anywhere.

This hype is all in the brochure, of course. But to quote Joseph F. Woodward in an article he wrote for the *L. A. Times:*

> Fifteen years in the making, Art City has evolved into a dynamic environment that allows artists to create in a supportive atmosphere.

Studio/Gallery hours are Wednesday through Sunday, 10 a.m. to 5 p.m.

All this seemed very positive. So why the feeling of impending doom? Perhaps an interview with the owner Paul Lindhard would explain it.

The first thing Paul did was give me a brief history of the area. It was once a thriving fishing camp. The June 15, 1878, *Ventura Signal* reported that Mr. Robert Ferguson and two companions caught thirty-eight-and-a-half dozen trout in the Ventura River last week.

Later there was a motel on the site. When the city condemned it to put up the river embankment, Lindhard bought the property and created Art City.

He also mentioned a man named Dubber, the first white settler in Ventura County who planted olive trees on the property that today is known as Dubber's Tract. It can be found at the south end of Highway 33.

A visit to the site of the Art City annex unveiled a tragic story and explained my uncomfortable feelings. Two fires had wiped out many statues, paintings, photographs, and one beloved dog.

The first was a propane fire in the kitchen of the complex, the cause of it unknown. The second fire was worse. Children were playing with matches beyond the fence where there were a lot of dry weeds. This fire spread quickly and burned up more studios and 50 of the owner's sculptures—the accumulation of nearly a lifetime.

Lindhard has fought back. Determined to provide a place where sculptors and other artists can work in a supportive environment, he carries on. A huge olive tree on the property planted by Dubber, which must be 250 years old, was nearly lost in the fire. But it is coming back too and is still producing olives.

I left feeling reassured; the negative vibrations I encountered would soon be displaced by happier ones.

The House with the Colorful Stones

Once upon a time there was a house near the 33 off-ramp with brightly colored stones in the front yard. As far as I can tell from the map, it was at the south end of Olive Street after passing under the 101 Freeway and before arriving at the railroad tracks, perhaps near the west edge of Front Street. It was a delightful sight, so unusual, and so out of the way as to qualify for one of the places to include in this book.

As the story goes, an African American woman lived there. At the time I didn't investigate, and when I went back to see whether the stones still existed, they were either gone or I had the wrong location.

What happened? I may never know. Did the owner pass over? Did the city object? The big rocks were near the street. Perhaps the property sold and the new tenants didn't like the colorful display. Some people have flowers in their yards; this person had something hardier—the brightly colored rocks.

I felt strange, as if I'd missed out on an opportunity to meet someone interesting, or someone who had an intriguing life or story to tell. It's much the same sensation as losing a loved one before you had the chance to tell them how much you cherished them and other things you wanted them to know. Like lost souls, the colorful stones have disappeared.

Lover's Triangle

The road from Ventura to Ojai and Santa Paula was called the "Lover's Triangle." Young people would take a buggy ride on this all-day trip over poor roads and clouds of dust, and if they were still on speaking terms at the end of the journey they were truly in love.

Though the roads are paved now, unwelcome spirits still hover about. It was on the gravel along the side of this highway where I was riding with a friend one day on his motorcycle when he lost control and we fell over. The bike landed on my ankle, bruising it badly.

CHAPTER TWO

WEST MAIN STREET

As we round the corner from Ventura Avenue to Main Street, originally called Camino Real, we turn west to Julian Street and find Patagonia. Whenever I have visited there I found children playing outside and contented looking employees sitting at picnic tables while on break or eating lunch. It's no wonder the place fairly bursts with good chi.

Patagonia

Nationally renowned as one of the best organizations in the country to work for, a look at the employees' benefits explains why. *The New York Times* cited it as a company that has shattered the "glass ceiling," an invisible barrier that stops women from advancing to positions of genuine authority.

A retirement plan, subsidized cafeteria, and health benefits greatly enhance the employment package, as does flex time which allows surfers or others who are lucky enough to live in this part of the country an opportunity to pursue sports and other interests. The organization also allows employees, with full pay, to work at other environmentally sensitive sites for a period of up to two months.

Terrific as these perks are, their child care program, the Great Pacific Child Development Center, is considered the best in the country. GPCDC includes an infant care room for children as young as eight weeks, a kindergarten, and rooms for toddlers in between. The Kids Club picks up the children at the end of the local school day and brings them back to the Center, saving their parents the worry about after-school care. Patagonia is a credit to our community and to our nation.

Proceeding eastward along Main Street we come to the old San Buenaventura Mission, guarded by a statue of Fray Junipero Serra, 1713-1784, the founder of the first California missions. Before getting involved with the historical sites to be found here we'll visit the Fourth of July Fair that takes place on Main Street, formerly Highway One.

Fourth of July Street Fair

The first 4th of July celebration was held in 1860 with Judge McGuire delivering a speech and Thomas Dennis, who had established the first lumber yard in town, reading The Declaration of Independence. No one gives speeches now. There are other forms of entertainment.

It is 10 a.m. as I hurry toward the merriment. Already parking is scarce and the sidewalks are crowded with people who anticipate what lies ahead.

A variety of music greets me and, near tree-shaded tables, I see dancers gyrating to the strains of Country Western. I haven't taken time for breakfast, so a complaining stomach dictates the first stop to be at one of the dozens of food concessions. Fortunately, I find Joannafina's where they are serving up homemade tamales.

"We have a complete Mexican food menu at our café on Seaward Avenue," a pleasant woman explains as she hands me a printed menu. "Today we're just serving tamales."

I sit down to enjoy the repast while I watch the dancers. Then I look for a rest room. Sure enough, there's a line of Andy Gumps nearby—clean, though there's no way to wash your hands unless you brought something with you. And, as always when I am in a portable toilet, I have horrible thoughts about what would happen if I dropped something important, like my keys, down the purple-colored hole. "Rested," I proceed eastward.

As always, I am fascinated by the vendors' creativity. Lovely paintings, handmade jewelry, silk scarves, and my favorites, painted signs with clever sayings.

 Forget the dog,
beware of the children.

I clean house every other day.
This is the other day.

The sun is getting hot so I hurry back to where the car is parked near the historic mission and its haunted plaza.

The San Buenaventura Mission and Mission Plaza

The Ventura County Museum of History and Art, located at 100 Main Street, is a haven for anyone interested in this city's colorful history. Charles Johnson, who describes himself as a librarian, not a historian, nevertheless has surely forgotten more about Ventura than some of the oldest old timers ever knew.

Adjacent is a park-like area graced by a Moreton Bay Fig Tree. Though it is huge, it is dwarfed by two pine trees across the street and just east of the mission, probably the tallest trees in the city. As the story goes, a sea captain planted them 100 years ago to use as masts for his ships.

I had never noticed the pine trees before, nor ever found a narrow passageway just to west of them known as Valdez Alley until I discovered the Convention and Visitor's Center at the corner of California Street and Santa Clara. The helpful staff provided me with a pamphlet entitled, *Historic Walking Tour Guide: Downtown Ventura*.

How surprising to see what I hadn't noticed before in the years I had lived here. I don't wish to dwell too long on the past, but before journeying forth, I wanted to explore Valdez Alley.

Valdez Alley

At the top of the Alley is a small brick building which looks like a horse, if one uses enough imagination. It was dubbed *El Caballo* by the early settlers. Originally it was part of a simple but effective aqueduct system. In the 1800s, after it was flooded out, it served as the city's jail. Surely it couldn't have been dirtier or smelled worse than it does now.

When the storm of 1862 ruined this aqueduct system, a man named Egbert, who had a spring just west of the Ortega Adobe, came to the residents' rescue. Charging four bits for a barrel—about $8 in today's economy—he provided water for the thirsty population.

The spring is now gone and no one knows the exact location of the life-saving source of water. The system of barreled water was used until 1873 when a new wooden flume was built by Chinese labor.

Sebastopol

There is a mystery about the location of the bones of a man named Dr. M. A. R. Poli, the first doctor to practice in Ventura and for whom Poli Street was named. It was on this street he built a large adobe house he called Sebastopol after the Russian fortress city which was then very much in the news.

Dr. Poli was killed in a fall from his horse while crossing a river near Stockton. When the body was brought back to San Buenaventura his good friend and relative by marriage, Angel G. Escandon, Ventura's first Latino Mayor, took charge. He refused to permit the dead man's friends and relatives to bury him because the estate could only be administered as long as the body was above ground.

As time passed the rumor spread the corpse was hidden in the attic of Escandon's Main Street adobe.

There is no record of Poli ever being buried, though it is speculated the remains were finally interred in the Mission Cemetery on a moonlit night.

Children believed that Poli's ghost haunted nearby Valdez Alley.

Chinatown

Descending from Valdez Alley we go south and east across Main Street to another favorite place, the site of the city's original Chinatown. Located on the Figueroa Street Plaza, where two sparkling fountains are connected by a tiled rivulet, all that remains of the once bustling Chinese Community called Sui Mon Gong by its residents, is a bright red door at the front of a narrow passageway with a sign above it that reads *China Alley*.

As this space is only one city block long it is difficult to imagine that a completely self-contained community with its own shops, businesses, rooming houses, and a Taoist Temple (Anglos and Latinos called it the Joss House) existed here.

Sing Key, owner of the American Restaurant, organized a volunteer fire department to fight fires in Chinatown, but they answered calls in other parts of the city as well. The city fire trucks often found upon their arrival the flames had already been extinguished. The Chinese volunteers marched in every parade, loudly cheered by all residents of San Buenaventura.

The efforts of Key's brigade is often cited as the reason this city avoided the kind of racial conflicts between whites and Orientals that occurred in places like Los Angeles and Rock Springs, a coal mining town in Wyoming with a notorious past. Coal mine owners in Rock Springs had imported cheap Chinese laborers, along with their wives and families, to work the mines. So outraged were the men who had lost their jobs, they herded the Chinese laborers into a mine and blasted the entrance shut, then deported the women and children to the West Coast. To this day the bones of these men lie beneath the streets of this rough and tumble western town.

Stories of laundry businesses in Ventura's old Chinatown were confirmed in 1992 when Pierano's Market was renovated and workers discovered a hitherto unknown *lavanderia* (laundry) with a 26 by 30 foot washing pool under the building. According to Charles Johnson, as the property where the Chinese lived became increasingly valuable they were gradually shoved westward and eventually dispersed.

The brightly painted murals on the side of the Peirano Building are typical of advertising in the early part of the century. A little farther south, on the other side of the plaza, is the A. J. Comstock Fire Museum.

The Carlo Hahn House

The Carlo Hahn House at 211 East Santa Clara is a restaurant with a sign on the front that says *The Landmark No.78.*

Owners Jorge and Darleen Ramierez are aware the building is haunted. According to the brochures they make available to guests:

> The Carlo Hahn House is the home of Rosa, a young daughter of one of the many Italian families that emigrated to Ventura County in the late 19th Century. Bound by customs of the day, Rosa was forced into a loveless marriage with a man much older than she. Unhappy and lonely, Rosa found solace in the company of a young Italian man. When her infidelity led to pregnancy, Rosa, acting in desperation, hung herself.

No one knows for certain where this happened yet few doubt Rosa has made the Carlo Hahn House her final resting place. Although spotted on numerous occasions staring longingly out of a round window on the second floor, she is most often seen on the staircase, walking mournfully in a long, elegant dress. Many also claim to feel her presence in the banquet room and women's rest room.

These ghost and goblin stories are a reminder of something Mike the trolley driver mentioned as he was taking me and some out-of-town visitors on a tour of the city. Immediately to the west of Figueroa Plaza on the grounds of the Mission Gardens there have been at least 50 confirmed sightings of a strange phenomenon. A man and a woman dressed in Victorian clothing walk toward each other, but never meet.

Strange? People's imaginations? Power of suggestion? Who knows?

The City of San Buenaventura, now called Ventura, is very old. Many people have died here. Spirits who have unfinished business on earth often come back to try to rectify things. Consider this story told by a woman who lived in an apartment overlooking Mission Plaza.

I was watching television one foggy evening when I became aware of a presence lingering in the doorway. When I glanced up I saw a man gazing at me with a loving expression in his eyes. He was entirely white, body, business suit, shoes hair, everything.

I wasn't frightened because the apparition looked so kind and because my dog was with me and seemed undisturbed.

As I rose and went toward him he turned around and walked down the hall into my daughter's bedroom where she was sleeping. I followed him, but he disappeared. Mulling over this strange intrusion later, I wondered if it was the ghost of my grandfather. When he was alive he worried about us.

I feel he came back to make sure his granddaughter and I were okay.

Returning to Main Street I stop in at my favorite thrift store. The only ghosts found here are the remains of clothing which, once cherished, were outgrown, disliked, or abandoned for some other reason.

The Coalition Thrift Store

As a thrift store buff, I have visited many. This is one of the best. As you enter you find the place busy almost any hour it is open, and heavily populated on weekends.

The Coalition profits go to help the battered women's and children's cause. Some secondhand stores—as they were once called—have names that will touch your heartstrings, but are privately owned.

I enter this place anticipating a great adventure and I am not disappointed. A pair of green shoes that fit perfectly have a Liz Claiborne label and cost $2.99.

The Dutch style jumper with the brightly embroidered pockets is $6.99, but still has a $69.99 price tag.

Not all bargains are so wonderful. Garments may not fit and there is nowhere to try them on unless you don't mind undressing in public or can put them on over your outer clothing. You can't return items for a refund, either. But who cares? Since you haven't invested much to begin with you don't mind donating them back.

Taqueria Vallarta

This restaurant with a sign that claims it serves *Authentic Foods of Mexico* escaped my attention until one day when checking out of the thrift store a woman came in and said to the cashier, "I don't know why anyone would ever eat anywhere else." Such an unexpected endorsement deserved attention.

Ami went with me, and we found it excellent, genuinely South of the Border, not the Tex-Mex served in many cafes. Then she told me a story about the previous owner.

"He was murdered about a year ago. The two men who did it were caught and are now in prison."

Why was he killed? She wasn't sure, but it seemed to concern money the victim owed someone. It was only supposed to be a kidnapping but something went wrong.

Rumors, stories, abductions, murders. It wouldn't be surprising to hear about a lynching, so closely are the city's spirits intermingled with the past.

Spears Saloon

The old Spears Saloon at 298 E. Main Street, once uninhabited and badly in need of repairs, is being renovated. It is heartening to see because many of the businesses are moving eastward, lured by the new mall. But it would be a shame to lose a building with such a colorful history. Once the second floor served as the first city hall, the proprietor serving the government officials beer during their frequent breaks from the tiresome business of government.

Top Hat

Perched at the corner of Main and Palm, this miniature café with a few stools outside the windows, has done a thriving business at the same spot for generations.

Headlining the menu is *CHARLOTTE'S FEATURE - Chili Dog*. It's inexpensive and it's good, too, as is all the simple fare. The Top Hat Special is a Double Cheeseburger. The most expensive item, Chicken 'n Fries, costs less than a ticket to a movie. And where else can you get a big bowl of chili for a dollar?

But don't let the Top Hat's innocent appearance fool you. This tiny eatery has a place in history, for it was the scene of the first murder case in the world in which DNA testing was used to solve a crime.

A former vagrant, motivated to improve his life, had been hired to clean the Top Hat after business hours. One night while working he was confronted by a knife-wielding woman bent on robbing the place. Though she succeeded in stabbing him to death, he resisted fiercely and ended up with some of her skin beneath his fingernails. It was the DNA evidence from her skin that convicted the woman, a known troublemaker the police were glad to get off the streets.

The Hartman Residence

Turning north on Palm Street we see two lovely old houses that are mentioned in the city's "Walking Tour" guide sheet. The Hartman residence is now a pricey restaurant called 79 Palm after its address.

The Newton Ranch House

The Newton Ranch House next door to the Hartman is now occupied by the Patrick Daniel Salon and Spa and *Aveda, the art and science of pure flower essence.* The House's brochure tells of former residents and architectural features but fails to mention that this land was located near the Bull Ring, a scene of carnage and death when bulls were pitted against raging grizzlies.

The Bull Ring

The Bull Ring was built between the mission church and what is now Ventura Avenue, with the wall of the old garden forming the south side of the square. Adobe homes were opposite on the north side. Posts, put up to the east and west, were tied with rawhide ropes to keep the animals in the arena.

A newspaper article found at the Mission Library has this to say about the area in the mid 1800s.

> It must have been a quaintly picturesque place in 1864, with its straggling rows of little adobe houses along both sides of the street from Palm to the river. The houses were set in and

out with no attempt at regularity.

The street itself was no better than a bridle path, unused of wheeled vehicles, for there was only the carata, a lumbering affair with two wheels of solid wood sawed from a tree trunk.

The only water was hauled from the river and emptied into a container at the gate and sold for 50 cents a barrel.

Phoenix Stables

Across Palm is a historic area called Phoenix Stables, the name derived from the fact the old stable, which was located nearby and built of wood, burned to the ground.

The owner, John Seely, rebuilt the stable on its present site from materials that would not burn. And as Phoenix, the fabled bird in Greek mythology, arose from the ashes of its funeral pyre to renew youth and beauty, so the stable rose from the ashes of its demise.

The entrance was high and without an arch or other obstruction above because some of the wagons, when heavily loaded, were extremely tall. Originally this place was built as a carriage house. In 1921 it was used as the county garage and in 1982 as the Old Town Livery. Now the tree-shaded square is surrounded by offices, restaurants, and a free kids' art gallery.

As I sat enjoying the ambiance, it was not difficult to imagine horse-drawn carriages arriving through the narrow opening, disgorging finely dressed ladies and gentlemen in Victorian clothing into the courtyard to attend a theatrical performance. Where the new offices are located there was once a theater.

A flyer from one of the businesses, Café Voltaire, advertised "The Bum Steers" and said the group would be playing there on Saturday. Did these musicians know that directly across the street, a century and a half ago, bulls instead of steers entertained residents?

The Voltaire's to-go menu was delightful. For starters they featured *Killer Nachos, Newton's Idea, EL ROJO, Gooey Mozarella, Ali Baba and his three dips, Hot artichoke dip, Specialties and Soups and Salads.*

Though Café Voltaire is no longer located here, this plaza is one of the coziest little out-of-the-way places in Ventura.

C.A.A.N. Thrift Store

East of here on Main Street new adventures await. Across the street is the recently opened Child Abuse and Neglect (C.A.A.N.) thrift store, an offspring to the Coalition Thrift Store a block to the west, and sure to someday be as delightful as its parent.

There is a shadow that hangs about this place, as it is the site of a business that has vanished. Beverly's was a fabric and hobby store where you could find acres of material and all kinds of crafts items. It had been open so long when the store finally closed down—out of frustration at the problems they were having, not a lack of business—it was like losing a special friend.

Located in an area that has long been a hangout for drifters and derelicts, Beverly's employees found they were vulnerable to shoplifters. When Farmer's Market, ousted by the new parking structure a few blocks away, moved into the lot at the back and Beverly's regular Saturday morning clientele had nowhere to park, the owners quit.

Ventura's idyllic weather attracts street people. Not without compassion do I say this is a tragedy, not only for the homeless, but also for the shop owners and others who have to deal with them. We may shake our heads about things that happened earlier in our history but are we ignoring some injustices occurring today? Although Ventura has shelters for some, many of the homeless people cannot be helped. Despite the problems we have, Ventura is the third safest county in the United States.

Main Street Mini Park

Next door to the C.A.A.N. store is a tiny parkway where people can sit and picnic or cut through to get to Santa Clara Street. Well maintained, this grassy spot is typical of recreational areas all over town.

On weekends people pitch tents and sell a variety of things from handmade crafts to psychic readings. Or they used to. This mini bazaar is another will-o'-the-wisp that has vanished, perhaps because some residents grumbled about the commercialism. I was disappointed because I found the vendors innovative. This is Southern California where the weather is almost always nice and people find creative ways to make a living.

Farmer's Market

Because of our year-round growing season, every Saturday, from 8:30 a.m. to noon, the downtown area hosts a Farmer's Market. It is a wonderful place, full of happy shoppers, music, and fresh produce, including beets, my favorite vegetable. Much as I enjoy this magenta colored vegetable, I rarely get the fresh ones, having discovered when I cook them I end up with beet juice in my hair, on my face, hands, clothes, and all over the kitchen. For other non-gourmet chefs like myself, a slick way to prepare them is to save the juice from jars of sweet, bread-and-butter, or dill pickles, dump in slices or chunks of cooked beets, and marinate overnight.

3 Star Books and News – Adults Only

The next stop, across Main Street from the Mini Park, is an adult bookstore that looks uninviting because their windows are always covered up. I hadn't the courage to go in until friends Jan and Polly went with me. Our presence seemed to unnerve the young man working there. What on earth could we want? We were obviously too old to be carded, but most of his clientele, a fair number who were browsing through the merchandise, are young men.

"We're just looking around," I said, when he asked if he could help us find anything. All manner of erotic tapes and cassettes were available to rent, and other interesting items were for sale. "Do you have musical condoms, or know where I could find them?" I finally asked.

The question surprised him. "A friend is looking for them to give to her golf buddies at their Christmas party as a joke," I explained. "We've searched everywhere we can think of, including the adult stores in Europe, and haven't been able to locate any."

"Where did she hear about them?" he asked.

"They were mentioned in one of the advice columns, with no information about where to order them."

"I've never heard of them. If you figure out where to get some I'd like to know."

I agreed, and since my friends and I found nothing else that interested us, we quickly left the dark interior and returned to the fresh air and sunshine on Main Street.

Ventura's First Post Office

The first post office, opened in 1862 at 377 E. Main, is now a shop called "A Touch of Class: Distinctive Home Furnishings." It still has cubbyholes on a wall in the back room where mail was delivered to box holders.

While examining them I had a feeling of destiny, as if someone or something was trying to get a message to me from the other side and I wasn't tuned in well enough to receive it. I have often had these feelings since moving to Ventura, causing me to wonder if perhaps I had lived here before, in another life, and was destined to return. Slightly discombobulated, I returned to my research, looking for clues.

The delivery of mail is credited with changing the name of San Buenaventura. The official reason the name was changed was because the Southern Pacific Railroad requested it so it would fit into their small, printed schedules. Old Timer, John Newby, who had once been a stagecoach driver, called a Jehu, tells a different story. He claims the Yankees changed the name because too much of the mail that was supposed to go to Ventura was mistakenly sent to San Bernardino.

The first postmaster, Mr. Volney A. Simpson, originated letter delivery in California by carrying letters in his stovepipe hat and handing them out when he met people in town.

Edie's Treasure Room

If you are serious about new age issues, stop in at 427 E. Main Street. Looking for crystals, runes, and books about astrology or Tarot cards? You can find them at Edie's. Recently emerged from a nearby mini mall, it is now on Main Street.

New age businesses, of necessity, must make money. But some of them are so intent upon making a profit much of the spirituality is lost. This is not true here, the exotic-looking owner is a genuine individual who cares about those who enter her establishment. Do you want something she doesn't have? She can order it for you or tell you where to find it.

This is the only place I have ever been able to buy Rider Waite Tarot cards in a size similar to that of regular playing cards. They are much easier for people to handle than the usual over-sized or undersized decks.

1-800-The Moon, the phone number for Llewellyn Publications, first surfaced at Edie's in the form of a catalog called *New World of Minds and Spirit* (NWM&S). Along with the hundreds of listings of books about Wicca, astrology or health foods, are fascinating vignettes that relate true happenings.

The story of a beekeeper who died at a time when bees rarely left their hives sticks in one's mind like honey.

The man loved his charges and they, in turn, loved him.

While mourners sat beside the open gravesite waiting for the casket to be lowered into its final resting place, they were startled by a strange humming noise. Swarming overhead in graceful curves, it became evident the winged creatures had left the safety of their combs to pay their final respects. As peacefully and mysteriously as they arrived, they returned home.

Another story in NWM&S told how to make Indian Prayer Sticks, with unexpected results. Fascinated by the power the simple sticks held to send prayers to Heaven, a wealthy woman named Helen began making them to give to her equally wealthy friends; those who "had everything" but needed spiritual help.

In each instance, after the slender sticks, decorated with paint or simple baubles, were placed in the earth so the feathers at the top could waft its owner's prayers upward, wonderful stories returned to the giver like bread cast upon the waters.

"It was the first thing I saw when I opened my eyes this morning," a woman engaged in a bitter divorce told her friend. "When I realized the feather was trying its best to answer my prayers, I knew everything was going to be all right."

A woman worried about a runaway daughter relates an equally heart-warming tale. "I decided to put my problems in the hands of a Greater Power. So, feeling silly, I stuck the prayer stick in the garden amongst the honeysuckle vines—my daughter's favorite flowers. A few hours later she called and asked if she could come home."

Edie is a cat lover, as many spiritualists are. A girl named Kitty told me this story.

"I arrived at my apartment after work one evening to find all three of my cats crouched, ears laid back, tails twitching, staring angrily at a table in a corner of the living room. Sensing a ghost was there, I rushed to tell Wanda, a neighbor who knows about such things, and implored her to see what she could do.

"Right away," she agreed and, upon entering Kitty's apartment, sized up the situation instantly. "Get out of here!" Wanda ordered the apparition.

As the cats stalked it down the hallway, the thing seemed to obey, then suddenly detoured into the bedroom.

"Don't go in there!" Wanda shouted. "Get out!"

She pointed to the closed door.

"And don't ever come here again."

Slowly the cats backed from the bedroom and faced the entryway, still angry. Then, just as suddenly, they relaxed.

"I'm sorry," Wanda said, "We had a séance in my apartment this afternoon and things got a little out of hand."

"Well, uh," Kitty stammered.

"Don't worry," Wanda said, smiling as she left, "He won't come back. I promise."

All this from a little shop on Main Street? Who knows when you set things in motion where the ripples will end. That reminds me of something else.

New Worlds of Mind and Spirits magazines began appearing in my post office box and continued for several months. I hadn't subscribed nor, until later, purchased anything from it. Perhaps Edie had ordered it for me or some psychic energy was responsible. Though I am quick to refer people to it who are searching for the type of information it contains, I may never know why I was the recipient of such a gift.

Anyone who wishes a reading can ask Edie. She knows most of the psychics in town and will give you a referral.

The Mini Malls

Next we explore two of the most hidden spots in town, the mini malls tucked away along the block of Main Street between Palm and Oak. The first can be found beside the Senior Craft Shoppe. It is an unexpected alleyway that reminds one of some of the narrow openings found in foreign cities like Bejing and London.

El Jardin Patio

The space at 451-461 E. Main is like an open sesame experience. Surely this is one of the loveliest commercial spots in the old city of Buenaventura. To quote from the walking tour guide:

> Entering the courtyard, shoppers feel as if they are in another world. Here is a fountain, flowering shrubs and pleasant nooks in which it rests, where shopping becomes a pleasure. It has retained its Spanish Colonial style with its raised courts, and wrought iron railings.

The brochure does not exaggerate. This alleyway is a joyful experience, full of good chi.

The Phantom Bookstore, (now an etching studio), owned by John Miller and Katie Crawford Miller, was located at the end of the mall. Here I found the book, *Erle Stanley Gardner's Ventura: The Birthplace of Perry Mason*, written by Richard Senate and illustrated by John Miller.

And so begins another trip down memory lane. As a book-a-day kid I haunted the library in the dusty little town where I was raised. I have always loved mysteries so imagine my delight when I discovered four books written by someone named Erle Stanley Gardner on the bottom shelf in the south wing of the building.

One I remember most clearly had the word *bride* in it: *The Case of the . . . Bride*. Sure enough, the fifth book Gardner wrote, in 1934, was *The Case of the Curious Bride*.

Gardner left his mark upon this city just as he left his mark upon my life. I read all the "Case of" books I could find, not realizing he had written many others. At the time I first discovered him, Perry Mason had not become the household word he is now. In a way I felt betrayed that millions of people liked him as well as I did. It was like discovering your lover has other women.

But I survived this trauma and today I am thrilled to realize I'm walking in places where Gardner walked. Not too far away, at the southeast corner of Main and California, is a building with a plaque on the side that says, *Perry Mason Was Born Here.*

It was dedicated by Gardner's wife, Jean, his daughter, Grace Naso and his secretary, Ruth Sophia Moore—not Della Street.

The law firm of Benton, Orr, Duval and Buckingham, on California between Main Street and City Hall, is one of many locations around the city where Gardner had offices. Indeed, he seems to have lived and worked in as many places as George Washington slept.

As the book progresses we will encounter Perry Mason's name and the influence he had upon our city many times.

Aphrodite's

It was one of those days when my aura must have been dark. Earlier I had put a guy off in one of the shops at the marina; then something I said offended Sandi and Lori, who own Aphrodite's. Once I was able to convince them I had only their best interests at heart, they explained a little about their business.

"We offer women a safe place to shop for unusual lingerie and other hard-to-find articles of clothing. This is a relationship enrichment center. We have a lot of high profile clients who aren't comfortable being seen in here. But they like our merchandise and they trust us, so they often order items by phone."

High profile or not, Aphrodite's is one of the "don't miss" shops on Main Street.

La Mer

At the top of Oak Street, majestically perched on a grassy knoll, is a lovely house with the intriguing name of La Mer; European Bed and Breakfast. To quote Elmer Dills, KABC-TV and Jerry Hulse, L. A. Times Travel Editor, the La Mer is the "Most Romantic European Getaway in Southern California."

Their brochure says,

> Nestled in a green hillside, the Cape Cod-style Victorian house overlooks the heart of historic San Buenaventura and the spectacular California Coastline.

> Originally built in 1890, La Mer has been faithfully decorated by host Gisela (pronounced GEE sell uh) Baida to create an old-world atmosphere.

> At La Mer each guest room has been furnished individually to capture the feeling of a specific European country. French, German, Austrian, Norwegian, and English-style accommodations are available.

> Rooms include complimentary wine and, as is typical of European bed and breakfasts, cozy European comforters. The cheerfully designed, antique-filled rooms have the distinct charm and personality of the country they represent. La Mer's is located only a few blocks from the beach and within walking or biking distance of Ventura's many shops, restaurants and other attractions.

Now let's take a short trip up California Street where our magnificent city hall with its marble walls is located and where, on Halloween, Richard Senate tells stories of the ghosts and goblins roaming through it.

City Hall

Tourist literature leaves out some of the more interesting facts when they extol the attractions of this beautifully located building with its sweeping vista of the coastline. Chief amongst these is that the place was once used as a jail, later the women's jail. In 1941 a woman inmate hung herself in her cell, using her bra.

More recently the space was used as an art gallery. Mysteriously, every morning one of the paintings hanging on the east wall was upside-down. This was near the site where a male prisoner trying to escape using a rope made of bed sheets fell to his death. His ghost is the one many believe is responsible for reversing the picture during the night.

Faces of Franciscan *padres* peer out at us from around the top of the structure until you arrive at the west wing. It was here prisoners were incarcerated before the newer jail was built on Victoria Avenue, and stories of hauntings abound. Sightings of a head floating around the council chambers is a reminder a judge once died during a trial.

Clusters of lima bean bouquets, like peace offerings, decorate the bronze gateways at the entrance to the building. Ventura was once the lima bean capital of the world.

The statue in the front of the building, ostensibly another replica of Fray Junipero Serra, was originally made of cement. Because of the salty sea air the nose kept falling off, so it was later cast in bronze and replicated in other locations. The identical statue can be found in at least twenty other places, three of them in this city.

This courthouse was where the infamous Elizabeth "Ma" Duncan case, Ventura's Trial of the 20th Century, took place.

Duncan refused to share her son with any woman. When he married she plotted to have his new wife murdered and hired two men to do the heinous deed for $6,000.

The night of November 17, 1958, they kidnapped the victim from her Santa Barbara apartment, planning to kill her and bury her in the deserts of New Mexico.

Unfortunately for them, they had car trouble. So after bashing in her head they buried her in a shallow grave north of Ventura near Casitas. The killers didn't get very far and, when captured, implicated Ma Duncan.

The trial was held in the County Court House, now City Hall, and the judge, Charles Blackstock, in an unprecedented move, permitted cameras in the courtroom.

Newspapers from all over the country covered the event. One of the facts that came to light during the two-month trial was that Ma Duncan had been married 20 times.

The jury brought in a guilty verdict and all three defendants were sentenced to die in the gas chamber. Duncan was the last woman to date to suffer the supreme sentence in the State of California. As an interesting side note, it was discovered that while on Death Row she plotted to poison one of the prison matrons.

Good Luck Talismans

A big well unearthed near the Mission yielded a large number of counterfeit coins, many of them Vietnamese, though it was long before that war. High in zinc and metal, people carried them as good luck talismans, though in reality their original purpose was probably as gambling tokens.

CHAPTER THREE

EAST MAIN STREET

Bonnie's

The warm rush of energy that greets you as you enter this place promises you're going to have a good time while you're here. Located at 532 E. Main Street, Bonnie's is one of Ventura's most delightful stores. Totally dedicated to parties and festivities, this shop has it all; hats, balloons, costumes, you name it, Bonnie's has it. And at Halloween it becomes a madhouse. A woman who worked there a while said, "For weeks you never walk, you run. It's fun, but it's exhausting, too."

I first met Bonnie at a garage sale where I was offloading some of my unwanted items prior to moving into a room in a house on San Clemente Street. Bonnie came into the yard searching for items to sell in her store.

What you notice first is that she wears a pendant with a large stone in it that looks valuable.

"It is," she explained. "People never used to pay attention to me. After I began wearing this bauble, they not only noticed me, they never forgot me, either."

Bonnie is a terrific person. Her store reflects her personality.

The Ink Shop

It was with some trepidation I approached the business located at 616 Main Street. It seemed to be closed most of the time. I was lucky enough to stop by on a day when the fellow managing it opened up and let me in.

The owner is George Christi, the same man who heads the Hells Angels' Organization. The tattooist is not a member of that group. His business card lists *Sterile conditions, New needles, Standard designs, Tribal designs, Custom designs, Body piercing and Cover-ups*, and promises privacy if the client wants it, but doesn't list his name. He specializes in eradicating unwanted tattoos, either by taking them off or going over them to turn them into something else.

You love Mary and have her name inked on or near your privates so it's there forever, then the relationship goes sour. As fate would have it, you fall in love with Kathy who knows Mary and hates her. So before you get too involved, you have to do something about it. Not to worry; this artist can turn Mary into a bouquet of flowers and Kathy will never know the difference.

At least she won't if you're able to stay cool long enough to wait for the repair work to happen before any real damage is done to your new relationship.

Once outside, I realize I have been holding my breath. Why? I shake off my qualms and head diagonally across the street to the Foster Library. It's one of my favorite hangouts. I know as soon as I enter I will find many "friends." At the top of this list is:

Erle Stanley Gardner

Born in Malden, Massachusetts, Erle emigrated west in 1899 when his family moved to California. He attended college but, according to *Times* staff writer, Gary Gorman, never graduated and passed the California bar without a degree in law or anything else.

Gardner first practiced law in Merced, then moved to Oxnard to escape the heat. Here, in one early case, he became a champion of the underdog representing members of the Chinese Community who were in trouble for running a lottery.

Faced with certain guilty verdicts and prison sentences, Gardner hit upon the idea of moving the defendants to different locations the day of their arrest. He was certain the warrants would be issued by addresses instead of recognition. And the ploy worked, just as it always worked in the stories he wrote. An angry judge had to release all the prisoners because the warrants had been served to the wrong men!

Gardner used to take coffee breaks at the Townsend Café which became the Busy Bee located next door to where Dexter's Camera, Hi-Fi, & Video Store is today. After the conclusion of a successful case, he had a steak, medium well, with a baked potato and garden salad at the Pierpont Inn. It was there he met his second wife, Jean, who may have been the model for Perry Mason's secretary, Della Street.

Gardner lived in five different homes in Ventura, the first at Main and Fir where the Rosarito Beach Café is located. The only residence left is at 2420 Foster Avenue.

I had a déjà vu experience there. It is a lovely area with a grand view of the city and seashore unfettered by trees or telephone wires. Researching the location, I realized I had been there before. I don't remember why, but do remember no one was at home. Eerily, it had nothing to do with Gardner because at the time I was not aware that it had ever been his home. A mystery, albeit a small one, that may never be solved.

His first Perry Mason novel, *The Case of the Velvet Claws*, and many others, can be found at the public libraries in the area, and were available at the Phantom Bookstore. The Millers have some first editions. One of them is the *Claws* mystery.

Gardner was not the only lawyer in Ventura to champion the underdog, there was also an attorney named William Edgar Shepherd. A role model for Gardner, Shepherd was so philanthropic that his wife, Theodosia Burr Shepherd, a distant relative of Aaron Burr, had to work to help support the family.

She became very famous for her horticultural efforts raising seeds on a small plot that is now the site of Foster Library. A Suffragette, Theodosia hired women laborers, mostly Chinese. Some of her plants can still be found in the parking lot at the back of the building.

Foster Library

A library holds the same allure for me a mermaid holds for a lovesick sailor. Once I pass through her doors I am in a land of enchantment. All those books, just for me, more than I could read in a lifetime. Since this library and I have become such good friends, I wanted to find out more about it.

Modern libraries are no longer set in park-like squares in the center of town as they were in yesteryears. This is no exception. It is named after E. P. Foster, an apricot rancher who donated $50,000 for the library and city hall, which was on the same site. He also gave San Buenaventura a hospital and park. The library was built in 1921 and renovated for the first time in 1959, and again in 1999.

An enlarged photograph in the meeting room at the west entrance shows Main Street as it looked in the early part of the century. The photo was taken before the De Leon Hotel at the corner of Main and Chestnut burned down, and shade trees outside the building welcomed those who entered.

The writers of many other mysteries—my favorite stories—can be found here. Beginning with the A's a few months ago, I discovered Steve Allen had penned several. Though his adventures were absorbing, what intrigued me most was that he has written and published more songs than anyone else.

How this process begins, according to Allen, is that the tunes spring upon him at unexpected times—when he is in his car waiting for a streetlight to change, or eating breakfast. At a loss to explain this phenomenon, he is as prolific a songwriter as Gardner was a crafter of whodunits.

I became a fan of Dick Francis and Sue Grafton when I discovered their books in my daughters' homes. Francis, a jockey who rode for the Queen of England, begins his tales with an intensity that holds the reader in its grip until the last page is turned. Grafton, who became famous for her alphabetically entitled adventures such as *A Is For Alibi*, and *M Is For Malice*, is equally compelling, though less violent. She mentions Fray Junipero Serra and some other 18th Century monks in her 1996 novel, *"J" Is For Justice*.

Mary Higgins Clarke, author of *While My Pretty One Sleeps*, *The Cradle Will Fall*, and dozens of other whodunits, is Vivian's favorite. Clarke was a stewardess before she married the boy next door, her brother's best friend whom she had known most of her life. But he showed no romantic interest in her until after she went to work for an airline.

Friends invited her to have dinner with them to celebrate her new job, and encouraged her to bring a date. Not knowing any-one else, she invited Clarke. After dinner, when he took her home, she asked him in to say good night and thank him for es-corting her. Instead of the expected friendly parting kiss, he be-gan making a list of names. When she inquired what he was doing he said, "I'm thinking of people to invite to our wed-ding."

Romantic? Indeed it was. Mary had been in love with him ever since she could remember. Unfortunately, he had a heart condi-tion that prevented him from buying life insurance, so she began writing mysteries to supplement their income. After his un-timely demise, Mary's books helped her support the family.

You will find romantic stories emerging from time to time in these pages. Mary's story is especially appealing to me, not only because I enjoy her books as much as the girls do, but also because I was a stewardess before I had my wings clipped and came back home to marry a boy I met at college.

The library has some unique services not everyone knows about. When I needed the correct spelling of the cat's name in the movie, *Bell, Book and Candle*, I asked the librarian working at the information desk. A few minutes later, when she called back, she told me it was Pyewacket, and seemed delighted to have been able to help.

Another service people are not always aware of is interlibrary loan. When I found a book called *Blue Roots*, published by Llewellyn, listed in *New Worlds of Mind and Spirit* catalog I wanted to read it without having to buy one. Could the library get it? It took a long time, but they obliged.

It is a collection of stories about the myths surrounding the Gullah people, written by Roger Pickney, published in 1998. Witch doctors, curses, cures and well-documented case histories come alive as the author pens the folklore of his childhood.

A listing of bad, unlucky signs follows with a warning to ignore them at your peril. But there are good omens, too, some easily heeded, especially if you can remember what you are supposed to say before you arise the first morning of every month.

Taboos, bad luck signs, and omens

Never:

♦ carry out ashes on Friday or between Christmas and New Year's Day.

♦ keep a crowing hen or carry a spade into the house.

♦ mend clothes while they are being worn.

♦ shake left hands as it will put a curse on both persons.

♦ start a new task on Friday or you will never finish it.

It is bad luck to:

♦ dream of chickens.

♦ walk backward or sleep with your hands clasped behind your head.

♦ lend matches or pay back salt.

(Hey! Wait a minute. In the next chapter there's a story about a woman who had bad luck because she *refused* to loan matches to someone.)

And more:

♦ A malfunctioning clock striking thirteen is a sure sign of impending death.

♦ If you start somewhere and have to go back because you forgot something, you must make an X in the road before you turn around.

(Boy, did that one resonate! I'm going to have to start making a lot of X's.)

♦ A hooting owl is a bad omen. Cross your fingers, take off a shoe and turn it over. Point your finger in the direction of the sound, put a poker in the fire, and squeeze your right wrist with your left hand. If you are barefoot outside, point your finger at the owl to cancel his power.

Good luck signs

♦ Dreams of gray horses mean an upcoming happy marriage while clear running water predicts good luck and money.

♦ If two people wash hands together they will be friends forever. Burning onion peelings afterward will strengthen the bond.

♦ If you see a red bird on your doorstep, count to nine and money will follow.

♦ Any bird singing on the doorstep means company is coming. The accidental dropping of a dishrag will hurry the arrival.

♦ "Hoppin' John" Black-eyed peas, rice, and ham boiled together and eaten New Year's Day New will bring a prosperous year.

♦ When you waken the first day of the month and say "rabbit" three times before you get out of bed it will be a good month.

♦ A piece of your lover's shirttail pinned to your skirt will keep him true.

♦ A strip of cotton tied around an ankle will keep cramps away from a swimmer.

♦ A bit of "magnetic sand" carried in a red flannel bag brings money and good luck.

♦ Wishes made to a new moon will come true, as will dreams beneath a new quilt.

♦ Bubbles in coffee mean that money is on the way.

♦ A nose full of snuff will quicken the labor of childbirth.

♦ The first water taken by a new mother must be sipped from a thimble. This will ease the baby's first tooth.

♦ Burn your old shoes and you'll never suffer snakebite.

♦ Burn your former lover's shoes and you will soon have more new lovers than you have time for.

♦ If you kill a snake in your yard, hang it from your porch post and your crops will never suffer drought.

♦ A knot of "five fingers" grass hung by the bed will make for restful sleep.

The Elizabeth Bard Building

Located at 121 N. Fir Street between Main and Poli, this former hospital is one of the most mysterious sites in the city. Now occupied by offices that enjoy a panoramic view of the coastline, it retains much of the spirit it had when it was occupied by the city's sick or dying.

Dr. Cephas Little Bard, who became one of the city's most beloved citizens, arrived in Ventura in 1867 and set himself up as a doctor. Thomas R. Bard built the hospital for his brother and named it after their sister, Elizabeth. Unfortunately, Cephas passed over before he was able to practice medicine there.

Like many hospitals, cemeteries and other places where people die, the Bard Building is inhabited by spirits. There was a morgue here, and one of the suites still has an attic with a dark stairway leading up into it.

According to Chuck Stauffer who has an office in the building, the producers of a show called "Sightings," broadcast out of a Los Angeles TV station that is interested in paranormal phenomenon, did a program about it when the programmers heard it was haunted. Whether it's haunted or not, strange things happen. Connie Lou Ornelas and Ross Hoffman who occupy a suite in another part of the building occasionally smell something weird.

"I thought it was someone smoking a pipe," Connie Lou relates. "Then one Saturday when only myself, my husband and our foster son were there, we smelled it again. Something or someone we couldn't see was causing that odor, and we were not sure what it was." (Unusual fragrances are often noticed by individuals dealing with ghosts or other unexplainable spirits.)

A doctor who has a clinic in the lower part of the structure had this eerie experience: Leaving the building after dark one night, two phantoms who looked like American Indians followed her to her automobile. Though she was alarmed, they didn't seem unfriendly and, as soon as she got in her vehicle and started to drive away, they disappeared.

Few occupants of the old hospital know the hill behind it was once an Indian village. People who live there report occasionally finding arrowheads.

This story brings back memories of a man named Paul Steward who used to hunt for arrowheads in the hills around Lamar, Colorado. Before he died he had a large collection.

I wonder what ever happened to that collection? It would be fun to see if any of the arrowheads matched the ones found in this faraway city by the Pacific.

Returning to Main Street let's visit a beautiful structure Erle

Stanley Gardner is credited with helping to build.

The Elks Lodge

B.P.O.E. stands for Benevolent Protective Order of Elks, or Best People on Earth, depending on who you ask. My experience with this organization inclines me toward the latter definition. Located at the corner of Main and Ash, this magnificent place with its welcoming Spanish style architecture and courtyard entryway came to my attention a few years ago when our bridge unit had to move the games out of the Masonic Temple.

The Elks welcomed us enthusiastically. Everyone was friendly, the building was gracious and, perhaps most importantly, there were four stalls in the women's restroom. The rent was low and downstairs there was a cozy bar where players could get drinks or sandwiches to enjoy during the games. It seemed like an ideal location, especially since it was near where we played before, and because parking was plentiful.

Unfortunately, we moved elsewhere. As this book is being written we may be on the move again. There are too many days at the church where we are located now when the space is unavailable. It won't be the Elks. Since they lost their license to run the card room, they may have to close their doors.

I have my fingers crossed this won't happen. If it does, let's hope the lodge is put to some other worthy use. It is such a lovely and historic building it would be a shame to have it vanish.

A Secret Place

This salon and day spa is tucked away at 739 E. Main, Suite B. Clients can partake of acupuncture and integrative medicine with James P. Rotello, M.A.L.Ac. His brochure says:

> If you are not satisfied with your present medical care and you would like us to evaluate your condition, we invite you to call for an appointment for your health and welfare.

That sounds good to me. I have long been of the opinion medical doctors ignore a great many things that can help heal the human body.

A Secret Place also offers massage therapy and Reiki with Ginny Winfield, Certified Massage Therapist. Her brochure describes Reiki thus:

> A treatment for stress reduction and relaxation that also promotes healing of body and spirit. It is administered by "laying on of hands" and is based on the idea that an unseen "life force energy" flows through us and is what causes us to be alive. If our life force energy is balanced, then we are more capable of being happy and healthy.

Information such as this always makes me wonder whether or not some of the horrific crimes people commit could be avoided if they had a few Reiki sessions.

Facial Treatments, Body Treatments and Body Waxing are available from Esthetician Jerra Myhre.

Do you suffer from unwanted hair? Cheryl Priamiano, R.E., California licensed Electrologist, promises she can free you of this suffering with permanent hair removal in the privacy and comfort of your own home, and her method of Thermolysis is FDA approved.

I don't know what the "R.E." and some of the other terms here stand for, but I'm not making fun of any of these professionals. I can clearly remember having a roommate with a lot of unwanted hair around her nipples who suffered terribly.

What intrigued me the most about this place, owned by hairstylist Trisha Cozzens, is its name. Tucked away in a spot that isn't noticeable, A Secret Place is a charming experience.

Ate Your Pager for $10

In the front window of a little shop that sells pagers and cellular phones, the eye-catching banner said, "Ate Your Pager For $10"

They must have meant "Activate Your Pager For $10" and something happened to the first five letters. Now the sign says, "Connect Your Pager For $10," but seeing the earlier message brightened my day.

Memorial Park

Known locally as Cemetery Park, this scenic hillside with a view of the Pacific Ocean visible through the branches of the trees is bordered by Main Street, Poli, Hemlock and Aliso.

It is another of the city's haunted sites. Sunny and occupied by day, residents rarely enter after dark. Little wonder ghosts reside here. When the gravestones were removed to turn the cemetery into a park, the bodies were left behind. Like those who have no address save a culvert or sheltering tree, they bemoan their fate.

A woman who lives in a home facing the park tells this story. "I had gone to bed, one of my cats in the bedroom with me, when I heard the other one run up the stairs. That isn't unusual as my two pets frequently sleep with me.

"Soon afterward I heard *another* cat run up the stairs and come into the room, then felt it jump on the bed. It was completely dark so I couldn't see anything, but since I was sure both of my cats were already accounted for, I decided to investigate. Just before I turned on the lamp I heard a cat running downstairs. My pets had heard it, too, because once the room was illuminated, I noticed both of them were staring at the door.

"I believe our invisible guest was a ghost cat, attracted to my aura because it knows how much I love felines. Or perhaps it was one that had been trying to visit a spirit in Cemetery Park and lost its way."

After visiting Cemetery Park one morning, I found a better reason not to walk around there after dark. So many people let their dogs run without picking up after them, your greatest danger is stepping in canine excrement.

We have two Congressional Medal of Honor winners buried here. General William Van Dever was with Sherman during his march on Georgia in the Civil War. His plaque reads "William Van Dever, BVT Maj. Gen. A Iowa Civil War. 3/17/17– 7/24/93."

Corporal James Sumner served his country in the bloody no-holds-barred Apache Wars of the late 19th Century. Though this forgotten hero was credited with saving his command, he later died in the Ventura County Poor House and, before being exhumed and interred in Memorial Park, was buried in "poor ground."

> *The grass grows quickly over the battlefield, over the scaffold, never.*
>
> —Winston Churchill

Mentioning the Medal of Honor to a friend who was helping me research the book, she said her husband, a career military man, had been awarded one. When I pressed her for details about what he had done to receive our nation's highest military honor, it turned out to be something else. "He has so many medals," she explained, "I get them mixed up."

San Buenaventura had its own version of an Indian War in 1819 when a group of Mojave natives came to the mission to trade, as they had for centuries. With a disdain for authority, they forced their way in. A scuffle ensued when the Spanish soldiers tried to disarm the Mojaves. One Chumash, two Spanish soldiers and ten Mojaves were killed. The mission dead were two lancers, Nicolas Ruiz and Miguel Cordero, and the Chumash neophyte, Jose de Jesus.

After the battle some of the soldiers and Chumash wanted the dead Mojave's heads cut off and displayed on poles as a warning. Fray Jose Senan wisely vetoed this barbaric idea and buried them in a mass grave near the beach, a gravesite that is lost to us today.

Tri-County Locksmiths

This little key shop, located on a point of land where Main Street meets Santa Clara, is included in this book for a very special reason. The owner has done me a favor. One time, when I asked him why I occasionally couldn't get my trunk open, he said the lock needed to be replaced. But then he told me something that saved me $20.

"If you turn the key to the right instead of to the left you won't have the problem."

I appreciated that. Sure, he could have replaced the entire apparatus; many locksmiths would have. But this guy took better care of me. The business has moved next door, but at least it hasn't vanished.

Billie Clower's Dance Studio

This dance studio at 75 S. MacMillan has an event you seldom hear about anymore. Every two weeks they have a cotillion for their young dancers—no grown-ups admitted. How appealing in this time of poor manners and other widespread social problems to teach youngsters the formalities of such an occasion.

I would have visited if I had been allowed. The owner explained that "the children act differently when their parents or other adults are around, so we don't let them attend."

Lee's Shoe Repair

This tiny place at 1806 Main Street is staffed by two individuals, Mr. and Mrs. Lee. He repairs shoes; she does alterations. What is most noticeable about this couple, aside from the fact they do good work, is that they enjoy each other. Walk in when they're not busy and you might find them playing a game or laughing together. They are also the ones who told me how to find the artist who painted the mural on the building next door owned by Pat Jump.

A Main Street Mural

Lisa Kelly's mural is a romantic picture of Fray Junipero Serra standing before City Hall, a blue stream of water—always a spiritual sign—behind him. Such a location does not exist in this city. City Hall is on a hill, the only thing behind it is more hill. The nearest water is the ocean which, though visible, is blocks away. Who cares? Like many of the anecdotes in this book, the artist created something from her imagination.

The Tree House

One day while walking along Main Street, which undulates and is therefore great exercise, I chanced upon a home on South Santa Rosa that had a little house in a big tree in the front yard. It also had a swing hanging from one of the friendly branches.

This looks like a home where children can grow up and play safely, where adults understand the need of their offspring for adventure and a place to call their own.

Meandering mentally back to my own childhood I see a small home with a big tree in the yard that had a Tarzan-vine-like rope hanging from it. Though mother knew where we were and what we were doing, the safety of this plaything was questionable.

We climbed a stepladder that was at least 12 feet high, jumped off clinging tightly to the rope and tried to seat ourselves upon the sturdy stick tied to the bottom so we could enjoy a ride out across the sidewalk, nearly out into the street. If you were unlucky enough to miss the crossbar you'd better hang on tight or you'd fall off!

Fortunately for me, the guardian angel that's hovered about me all my life never allowed this to happen.

Years later I heard a neighbor was so frightened by our daredevil antics she moved away!

Yon Hui's

Upon entering this sunny establishment at the corner of Main and Seaward, you are invited to seat yourself in a small area furnished with comfortable sofas and tables.

An attractive Asian woman waits on me and, when I explain that I'm looking for a denim shirtwaist dress, finds a reasonable facsimile. Since I'm shopping for a friend I don't buy anything, but leave with a good feeling.

If you're looking for some unique clothing try Yon Hui's.

Pacific View Mall

Don't fail to visit the great new mall rebuilt in 1999 at Mills Road between Main Street and Telegraph Road. Malls are the "in" places for people of all ages in our society today. Walkers inhabit them early in the morning because the floors are level and the weather is never a problem. Teenagers meet their friends there, others go to spend pleasant hours in a safe environment.

Waldenbooks

You will enjoy this bookstore which is located on the upper level of the mall. Their monthly newsletter, *Walden Book Report*, is free and as enjoyable a read as the novels they sell. The staff members are super nice, too.

Michael's Shopping Center

Near the east end of Main, this pleasant area is crowned by Michael's, a crafts store. Catering to the creative individuals in the community, you can find things to satisfy the urge for self-expression.

Oroweat Outlet

Our next stop is a discount bakery outlet. Oroweat has day-old products discounted by one third to one half, and sale days. A card you can get punched 10 times, for ten dollars worth of purchases, qualifies the customer for a loaf of bread courtesy of the store. A ten percent discount is given to senior citizens. If they fail to give you a receipt, your purchase is free. In the outlet's own quiet way, there's lots of hoopla, and some of the best bread in town.

Kinko's

At the east end of Main Street is one of those businesses you find excuses to patronize because you feel good while you're there, and because there's always something going on, even in the middle of the night.

Kinko's was named after the originator whose nickname was Kinko because he has kinky hair.

I can remember many years ago, when I first found it, Kinko's was operating with one or two copiers and beating the prices of every other print shop in Ft. Collins, Colorado.

When I moved to Ventura I discovered the originator once resided in Santa Barbara and started his operation there. Eventually he moved the international headquarters to Ventura.

This huge organization has not lost the personal touch. You go into this roomy place that is always open and find it's staffed with helpful people who do an excellent job.

I have often been lured away by cheaper printers, only to return to Kinko's.

Office Depot

In the same shopping center as Kinko's, Office Depot is another outfit that does an outstanding job. This company never has sales because, as one staff member explained, it sells products at bargain prices all the time. It also has a duplicating service snuggled into the corner that has the best prices on copies I've been able to find anywhere in town.

Barnes and Noble Bookstore

Ventura was lucky to get this upscale bookstore. When it was in Santa Barbara I would stop in whenever I had time because there was always something fun going on. If it wasn't a book signing or entertainers, it was people reading something they had written. And now we have them in Ventura.

There is a quiet area where you can have a cup of tea and settle down to read, or rest, or people-watch.

If you're a book hound or just want to browse, don't miss Barnes and Noble.

Stagecoach Driver, Nephi Jones

The American Hotel on the corner of Main Street and Ventura Avenue was the depot for the stage. Stagecoach driver Nephi Jones, the town's first Mormon, would always blast his trumpet when he came across the river into San Buenaventura, even if he arrived after midnight.

CHAPTER FOUR

THOMPSON BOULEVARD

Thompson was originally named Meta, which means "goal" or "finish," for the annual horserace held on San Miguel Day. If it were longer it surely would have at least as many spirits hovering around it as Main Street for it is closer to the sea.

The name of this thoroughfare was changed to honor "Dixie" Thompson who trained horses to dance and was a featured participant in every local parade. Spectators at this festival were also treated to bull fights, bull and bear battles, and a rodeo.

The Meta Motel at the corner of Figueroa is one of the few reminders of the original name. Cattycorner across from the Meta is a tiny business that stirs my imagination every time I see it.

Tony's Pizzeria

This miniature pizzeria, which looks like a hut tucked away in a tropical forest, is almost hidden from view in this jungle setting. I listen for Cheetah chattering away in the trees, warning Tarzan that if he doesn't soon swing into the clearing to save Jane, some dire fate awaits her. Sometimes on Saturday nights if you listen closely you may hear the electrifying yodel that means he is on his way. Or is that just the noise of the stock car races coming from the nearby fairgrounds?

Whether this place fires your imagination or not, the pizza is terrific, the service great, and the setting lush.

Book Mall of Ventura

On the sunny corner of Oak Street and Santa Clara is a bookstore with a sign overhead that says, *Spiritual readings, Tuesday, Wednesday, Thursday, Friday and Saturday.* The Book Mall used to be on Main Street but a fire forced them to this new, very inviting, location.

Outside is off-street parking. Inside, in addition to a huge inventory of books, there's a friendly, helpful staff, and a room where people can hold meetings. At night? That's all right, they are happy to accommodate you.

The uniqueness of the place was the secret door. Looking like a tall shelf filled with books, if you knew where to press a certain lever, you could open it and go into another room. This is written in the past tense because it has disappeared.

The first time I saw the secret room it was dark and full of packing cases. Now it is filled with bookshelves and light. If you find something you want to peruse you are welcome to do so in the adjacent meeting room, invitingly furnished with couches, chairs and tables.

Lu Ross Academy

Lu Ross Academy & Salon & Wellness Spa at 470 Thompson Boulevard is one of those good energy/chi places. You can tell as soon as you enter something nice is going to happen.

It is a beauty school where students are trained in cosmetology and other specialized fields. Many of them are young women with magenta-colored hair. There are a few male students here and some older individuals who are entering the job market late in life or undergoing a career change. A sign at the entrance announces that all the work is done by students.

You see both male and female clients. Gone are the days when a guy wouldn't dare to be seen in a beauty shop. Now they are getting perms, haircuts, and manicures just like the women. Some of the spa packages are available for couples.

Lu Ross offers a breathtaking variety of services. To name just a few, there are body massages, spa body therapy, herbology wraps in hydro-active mineral salt, aromatherapy wrap, body waxing for those who wear bikinis, and body works with a facial for the back (How do you give a facial to the back?)

They do hair, too. Deep conditioners and scalp treatments are available, as are perms, color treatments, and cocktail manicures for fingers and toes. Their gift certificates say, *The best gift is a gift of health. Give it to yourself and your loved ones.*

Except for the two-and-a-half hours it took a new student to shampoo and cut my hair, my experience with this organization has always been good.

The staff at Lu Ross does a fine job training their students in public relations. They are unfailingly polite and considerate and almost always do excellent work. Not only that, senior citizens get a 10% discount.

El Nido (The nest)
On California Street next door to the Bella Maggiore, which means Beautiful Old Thing, was the Astor Hotel. It was one of many sleazy places in this part of town, and another where a murder occurred. (There have been so many murders mentioned in this book it is beginning to sound like a Perry Mason novel.)

"Be her careful what you say about it," cautioned Helen, the friend who told me the story. "Her daughter still lives here and wouldn't appreciate the publicity."

The victim, who was working at the hotel at the time, was not killed by a spouse or lover, but by a stranger who stopped in to ask for a book of matches. He was a former patient who had been released into society when many mental institutions were closed. Enraged when the woman explained that she didn't smoke and didn't have any matches, he bludgeoned her to death.

Our perception of these hospitals is highly influenced by movies such as *One Flew Over the Cuckoo's Nest*. A first-hand account from a man who has been a "guest" on many occasions, tells a different story. According to him, life is very pleasant. You are safe, the food is excellent, and the staff kind and helpful.

Turning Point Foundation

A sweeping view of the Channel Islands and Pacific Ocean makes the 101 Freeway off-ramp at Thompson Boulevard one of the most beautiful in the world. Near the base is a fine example of Ventura's efforts to help those in need. The Turning Point Foundation is a shelter where the mentally challenged can find a safe haven until they are well enough to manage on their own.

The Mitchell Block

This block is lined with stately houses that are so old they look like they are—or should be—haunted. Literature available at the visitors' center recounts their history. Walking along here is an enchanting experience.

Fortunately, most of these mansions have been turned into offices and commercial buildings, otherwise they might have fallen into disrepair. Only one looks like it has anyone living in it, and one is empty.

I stood beside the For Sale sign, envisioning what had gone before. It must have been a family home as it had three stories and many rooms. It also had a grand view of the ocean.

Erle Stanley Gardner often took his wife and daughter to this beach and camped out for days at a time. The children who lived in these homes could run to the water's edge and play within sight of anyone gazing from a back window.

These "Painted Ladies" activated my over-active imagination. I wanted to buy the big house, fix it up, and live there. It's a wonderful location, directly across the street from a park.

Plaza Park

It is difficult to figure out why some parks are inviting and some are not, but this is definitely one of the former. Bordered by Thompson Boulevard, Santa Clara, Chestnut, and Fir Streets, this grassy recreational area is graced by a magnificent fig tree which a plaque describes as a Ficus Macrophylla Fig, Moreton Bay Australia, 1874. Over 73 feet tall, it has a leafy branch spread of 139 feet.

It is an impressive sight, but the most wonderful thing about it is the hospitality offered. Those who sit or sleep under its branches are afforded shade and some protection from the wind and rain.

Just south of the fig tree is a new structure holding clean restrooms. There used to be a low hill on this site with a bench where people could sit and enjoy the shade. During a period of renovation the mound was leveled and the new building erected. Though it is an improvement on the facilities, it's too bad they had to get rid of the hill, for it was a good vantage point from which to watch what was going on in the park.

There is a playground with swings, slides, a seesaw, a small push-me carousel, and lots of children and mothers, a fair number of fathers, and baby strollers. On the east edge of the park is a new gazebo. Built in 1999, it is the third such structure in the park's history.

During WWII, bond drives like the ones held in Plaza Park financed 50 percent of the war effort. A little-known fact about WWII was that there were fully half as many casualties on the home front as in the battle zones. In addition to the death rate from normal causes such as illnesses, there were many accidents in defense plants. In our zeal to make the equipment our fighting men needed, safety was given a low priority.

Scattered around the grounds are tables where people can have picnics or outdoor meetings. Not too long ago we had First Sunday in the Park. Venders set up tents and booths and sold their wares. It was a delightful occasion, now just a thing of the past, another ghost to enrich our memories. Yet Plaza Park is still what every park should be, a place where young or old, rich or poor, residents or guests, can enjoy themselves.

The Magnolia Tree

Travelling east on Santa Clara, next door to the Leewood Hotel, is another magnificent magnolia tree. A sign says the Pacific Telephone Company went to some trouble to save it when they built the parking lot behind it.

I'm carried back to nights when, as a teenager, I went to proms and my escorts bought me magnolia corsages. I couldn't have imagined being able to pick them from a tree.

After sundown this tree has a darker aura. Once, walking beneath its branches near midnight, I heard noises that sounded like people muttering. Unable to identify the source of these strange sounds, I hurried away.

Insane Clown Posse

The instant I saw the Oregon license plates and the legend on the front of the bus parked at the corner of Thompson Boulevard and Fir Street, I knew that conveyance was going to disappear. Decorated to look like it was being consumed by fire, the bus provides shelter for a traveling rock group. They were in Ventura only briefly, on their way to another destination.

The Rose Wall

The home at 871 Thompson has a wall in front decorated with breathtakingly beautiful roses. It's a treat to see when rounding the curve from downtown.

Five Flags

977 Thompson Boulevard is a house where a great deal of creative decorating is taking place and a delightful energy envelops passersby. The gate that leads into the back yard has cutouts of animals. The railing around the balcony upstairs looks like a picket fence. The flags of Canada, New Zealand, The United States, Greece, and California fly from it.

Searching for the story here, I found the owner at home one day. His motivation? He likes to do carpentry work. Obviously a labor of love, this is one of the must-see homes in town.

The Rooftop

Journeying eastward on Thompson you reach Laurel where an innovative sight appears. Perched atop a pointed roof, a deck chair faces the Pacific Ocean.

To date no human occupants have been spotted. But what a great way to enjoy one of the earth's most spectacular views.

The Wharf

On South Laurel, beside the railroad tracks and very near the ocean, is a business called, The Wharf. Their brochure says

> Make the Wharf your source for great gifts, Western and Ranch Wear. Located near Ventura's historic Old Town at Front and Laurel Streets, we invite you to drop by for a visit. Your trip to Ventura would not be complete without it.

As I leave I think how aptly named the place is. I also have a feeling there is a life force here that can't be explained by the factual information in their literature. Perhaps it is the energy that rolls off the ocean's waves as they throb against the shore.

Wine Lovers

Tucked into a shady nook at 1067 Thompson Boulevard, this is a place for lovers to rendezvous. Once a domicile that housed a Tarot Card reader, the building has been transformed into a hideaway romantic enough for any liaison. Bright orange leaflets outside the entryway list a schedule of coming events.

> CHEERS! If you haven't made it down on Wednesdays, you're truly missing out on the best gourmet pizzas and calzones in the world! First of all, they're free (with the purchase of any wine or beer by the glass.) Second of all, we cook everything right there, including the dough, in our three roaring honeycomb fireplaces with oak which adds tons of flavor.

JoAnn and I accepted their invitation one Wednesday and were delighted. As we gossiped and drank beer and wine and watched the chefs baking small pizzas, we were protected from the noisy rush hour traffic on Thompson by stacks of firewood, a tall stone fence and tropical foliage. I felt as if I had discovered a secret getaway in the midst of a busy town.

The brochure goes on to advertise other activities for singles or those who want to be. There is a club that meets every Sunday from 2 to 6 p.m. with no cover charge.

In these days of computer dating, Wine Lovers offers a refreshing alternative. The ambience is friendly and the owner pleasant, helpful, and knowledgeable. Whether married or single, try it.

Café Z

Café Zack, next door to Wine Lovers, is open for lunch and dinner. They serve meals in a pleasant, unhurried atmosphere. This restaurant made it into the book because of their unusual name and gourmet cuisine.

Terry Lumber

This is a good chi lumberyard where you can go in and be waited on by someone who knows right where to find what you want—a real plus for women like myself who feel lost in the big discount lumber yards and hardware stores. They also provide a service I have found useful on several occasions. You are welcome to help yourself to any of the boards and other remnants outside in their scrap pile.

Bayview Automotive

In case this looks like just another small garage, be aware that looks can be deceiving. It's a business where the owner, Harold Stephens, and his employees, are dedicated to providing excellent, caring service at fair prices.

The Underground Rivers

Waiting for my car to be repaired one day in the parking lot at Bayview, I found a man dipping a small receptacle into a hole in the ground. Occasionally he would lift it and dump the muddy water it held into a bucket, then dip again. When I asked what he was doing, he said he was checking the water in one of the city's underground rivers.

One of our underground rivers!?

Water is one of the most spiritual signs in the psychic universe.

I knew we Venturans were beside a huge body of it but had no idea we were floating on it, too.

"How many do we have?" I asked, fascinated.

"Five."

"So why don't we get washed away into the ocean?"

He didn't know, but seemed unconcerned. He did point out, considering how dirty the water was, it made a good case for not drinking what comes out of the taps.

Cucina D' Italia

One of the nicest dining out occasions in Ventura, especially for those who enjoy Italian food, can be found at the corner of Thompson and Chrisman. The Cucina d' Italia Restaurant is in an old house, one of those comfortable domiciles where, upon entering, you get a sense of history. A family once lived here. They must have been happy because that feeling surrounds you.

The place delivers exactly what the exterior suggests—homemade Italian food in a friendly, domestic atmosphere. Don't bother making reservations because they are not accepted. You show up Wednesday through Saturday from 5 p.m. to 9 p.m. and take your chances.

The wine list, though short, is excellent. Upon being served you discover the salad is crisp, the bread crunchy, and the food just like you remember Mama made when you were a kid.

Hungry Howie's

Located at 1504 East Thompson Boulevard, the sign on the front says, *Nobody gives you choices like Hungry Howie's!*

A friend told me they make the best pizzas she has ever eaten, so I decided to see for myself. Because of the variety they offer and, especially, their flavored crusts, my friend might be right.

When I was a child no one had ever heard of pizza. Now I don't know how we'd get along without it.

Tender Life Maternity Home

Just east of Howie's is the Family Associates Clinic and the Tender Life Maternity Home. The former frequently has protesters, mostly men, picketing outside.

The only time I had occasion to visit the maternity home was the morning they had a rummage sale. The front yard was filled with a jumble of clothing and household items and young mothers carrying adorable infants. Babies bring so much joy into peoples' lives it is difficult to imagine how we could ever live happily without them.

Ventura's history as a fruitful place for married couples because of the climate and drinking water was mentioned in several newspaper articles found in the library at the Ventura County Museum of History and Art. One tells about a couple named Carr, barren for 12 years, who produced five babies in two years after moving to San Buenaventura. Other stories aren't as humorous.

In a speech given by Dr. C. L. Bard he relates how birth control was frowned upon and miscarriages regarded with disfavor. Missionaries punished women who had suffered this misfortune by shaving their heads and flogging them. They also forced them to sit in church several Sundays in a row holding a hideously painted doll in their arms.

Waters from the springs were also used to treat rheumatism. It contained asphaltum, which is found nowhere else on the continent, and sounds more like something that you would put on streets instead of on your body.

Eucalyptus Ficifolia

Another red underline appeared on the computer on the word, Ficifolia, but the man at the Green Thumb Nursery assured me it is the correct spelling. If you are in this lovely city during the summer months, driving along Thompson Boulevard to where it T's with Seaward Avenue, you will be treated to a spectacular sight. Huge bushy trees ablaze with beautiful red blossoms welcome people to our city. These trees grow all over town, but rarely in such abundance.

One of the things I have always loved about Ventura is the flowers that flourish year round. When I lived in Colorado, Wyoming and Utah I always had to beg them to bloom, coaxing them along with compliments and more tangible forms of fertilizer. Even then they came forth only in the warm months of summer. To find flowers always growing wild and blossoming in great abundance everywhere is heavenly.

F & M 98 Cent Store

At the corner of Hurst and Thompson is a place where most of the merchandise costs ninety-eight cents or less. According to my enthusiastic neighbor, Animal, "You can buy fresh eggs there and everything."

Wandering through it reminded me of the days when five and dime stores were popular. Ten cents purchased quite a bit in the thirties. Taxes were collected in tokens and ten tokens were worth one cent.

Mother was upset about pork chops because the price had gone up. "It's just like eating nickels," she grumbled. Her unhappiness was understandable. Dad, a house painter, never had any work in the wintertime. In fact, until World War II came along, and people had more money to redecorate their homes, our family was very poor.

The Perry Mason books are a gentle reminder of those days, for most of them were written during the Great Depression. Whenever Mason left a quarter tip, the waiter was thrilled.

Will a quarter buy anything at the ninety-eight cent store? See for yourself. You might be pleasantly surprised.

The Yellow Duplex

On Hurst, between Thompson Boulevard and Main street, is a cheerful yellow duplex. Once again I'm carried back to my hometown and my father, Gomer O'Dell. Over time he acquired quite a few properties in this prairie town, and he painted them his favorite color, yellow. You could always identify the houses dad owned because they looked like sunshine.

Pacific Avenue

The next place we visit is a fluke, somewhere I never would have found except for an unseen force that pointed me in that direction.

Stretching only two short blocks between Main Street and Thompson, Pacific Avenue is lined with shady residences whose spick-and-span yards are decorated with live flowers. It can be found between MacMillan on the west and one of the city's "lost" alleys on the east. It is typical of many small, residential areas where the Venturans take great pride in their homes and yards, and is like walking in wonderland.

Lost Alleys

Checking out the alleyways near Thompson Boulevard, I encountered a mixed energy. I call these alleys "lost" because there is no logic to their locations. San Miguel Alley, just east of Pacific Avenue and west of Santa Rosa, is the same length as both streets and runs in the same direction. Yet the city map identifies it as an alley.

At the south end, near Thompson, San Clemente Alley first appears at right angles to San Miguel Alley, then cuts across Santa Rosa Street to Santa Cruz. All this takes place several blocks west of San Clemente Street. Even more illogically, San Clemente Alley jogs north up Santa Cruz a short distance and finishes at Anacapa.

Earlier in the book a historian was talking about how the houses were built haphazardly with no regard for streets or other by-ways. This is the feeling you get when trying to make sense of the location of these wayward alleys.

The Development House

Property has become so valuable in the area it is not unusual to find houses built toward the back of city lots. Such a place was discovered at 165 Santa Rosa while I was checking out the alleys. Set well away from the street, this home has a tiny room perched atop the second story with a commanding view of the neighborhood and, in the distance, the ocean. What fun it would be to live there.

Fuller Paints

This store, where you can purchase paint of any color and the things you need to apply it, recently acquired a rainbow exterior. Stripes of many shades and hues greet you as you drive or walk toward the corner of Santa Cruz where Prince Alley begins.

Yellow, hot pink, and blue are followed by purple. These colors denote intellect, love, health, and purity, in that order. The owners avoided red which is a spiritually jarring color and the cause of so much stress at Christmas time.

We skip a few blocks now because Prince Alley, which stretches immediately south of Thompson between Santa Cruz and Coronado Street, is the subject of the next chapter. That brings us to blossom-lined Seaward Boulevard and a store whose business is parties.

Mr. Suds

Just east of Seaward Avenue, at 2343 Thompson, Mr. Suds offers more than the usual party balloons and supplies. The owners will also teach you how to make your own wine or beer and will sell you the equipment needed to do it.

The Magical Bird Spirit Tree

Directly across Thompson Boulevard from Mr. Suds is a globe-shaped tree filled with magical spirits. Whenever I walk by near dawn I hear the twittering of what sounds like hundreds of birds, yet not one leaf moves.

Going a little further east of this magical tree on Thompson, is a small shopping center that has two places worth patronizing. Eating establishments nurture more than our bodies. Whoever created the phrase "soul food" wasn't kidding. Anytime you happen on one that makes you feel good as soon as you enter, you have discovered a treasure.

Anacapa Bread Company

If you are fortunate enough to be in the area early in the morning you may suffer hunger pangs caused by the fragrances wafting from its open door. The time I was there they had just taken fragrant mounds of Honey Whole Wheat bread from the ovens. I bought a loaf and had eaten several chunks before I could get home and put butter on it.

All their fare, their sandwiches, loaves of bread, soups and salads are made fresh daily.

The Cottage Café

Near the end of Thompson Boulevard is the Cottage Café. It deserves four stars for treating kids like real people. They offer children's meals described as "Oreo Adventures," pint-sized servings with pint-sized prices. For breakfast you have a choice of one egg and potatoes, or one "face" pancake and egg, or two slices of French toast, or half a waffle.

Lunch choices are half a grilled cheese sandwich, or a corny dog, or peanut butter and jelly sandwich, all served with fries. For dinner the menu offers the youngsters a choice of chicken strips with fries and a veggie or ground beef patty and mashed potatoes with gravy plus a veggie, or a fish patty, fries and coleslaw. All meals are served with Oreo Cookies!

The adult menu is equally innovative. The waiters are pleasant and everyone is eager to please, so you enjoy excellent service with a smile.

Movie Stars

Legendary figures of the stage and screen have so much hype surrounding them it is difficult to separate the good guys from the bad ones. Everyone thought Joan Crawford was a saint until her daughter wrote *Mommy Dearest,* so how are we to tell them apart?

Who cares? If you like an actor and wouldn't miss one of his or her movies, it doesn't matter. The magic they project enables us to create our own perfect world, at least for a couple of hours.

There have been several occasions when movie stars visited the city. In 1927 football legend "Red" Grange (the Galloping Ghost) made a silent film in Ventura entitled, *Racing Romeo.* It co-starred the comic Walter Hires and popular actress Jobyna Ralson.

Another race car thriller, *The Crowd Roars,* starring James Cagney, was filmed at the fairgrounds in 1931.

Silent screen actress, Theda Berra (the Vamp), best known for her portrayal of evil women, once spent the night at the Ventura Hotel on Main Street.

Tragic silent actor, "Fatty" Arbuckle, was caught speeding down Main Street in the late 1920s. When he was ticketed he said that he had briefly lived in downtown Ventura on Junipero Street.

With the advent of talkies many silent screen stars faded from sight, their voices so horrific they couldn't survive.

Clark Gable was in town, but not to make a movie. According to an Oxnard gun shop owner, Gable was hunting ducks, poaching on the Fleischmann Estate, now the Olivas Park and Golf Course. Gable was almost caught by one of Major Fleischmann's outriders, but managed to get away with a few ducks.

Those movie stars are not the only ones that have been in town. Recently Julia Roberts' movie, *Erin Brokovich,* was filmed in the residential area behind Von's Grocery Store at the five points area where Thompson Boulevard, Main Street, and Telegraph Road meet. The location had been chosen because the house and neighborhood matched the description in the script.

Because of Ventura's proximity to Hollywood, stars cross our path frequently. Many of them have homes in Ojai and Santa Barbara. Although I think I once spotted Gene Kelly at the Marina with a little girl who was riding the carousel, to date I haven't discovered any stars residing here. Too bad, it would be fun to have a couple around.

Death of a President

The first United States president to visit this city was William McKinley. In 1901 as guest of Senator Thomas R. Bard, he rode in a parade that stretched from Kalorama to Santa Clara and Ash, then up Main Street to the Mission where all the bells were rung at the same time. Five months later, when McKinley became the second president to fall victim to an assassin's bullet, he was deeply mourned in San Buenaventura.

CHAPTER FIVE

PRINCE ALLEY

Teeming with activity, this four-and-a-half-block-long passage between Thompson Boulevard and Ocean Avenue stretching between Santa Cruz and Coronado Streets has been given a royal name for reasons that have been lost in the mists of time. The marine layer lies heavily on this part of the city, so this visit includes all the businesses along this part of Ventura Boulevard, and many of the homes adjacent to Prince Alley.

It begins with a house facing Santa Cruz where a bougainvillea vine flaunts bright red blossoms almost two stories high all year long. At least it used to. It disappeared before I got to Prince Alley, as First Sunday in the Park did just before I got to Plaza Park.

Unlike the First Sunday event, the bougainvillea vine is not dead but trimmed back so it wouldn't take over the homeowner's entire yard—probably too so people could more easily drive vehicles through the narrow passageway beside the house. With our Mediterranean climate, plants grow in such abundance they must be kept in check.

The computer kept complaining about the way I spelled bougainvillea, so I looked up the spelling in my Webster's Dictionary and couldn't find it. I finally had to go to the library and ask for help from the Information Desk.

I sometimes walk my block of the alley between Santa Cruz and Anacapa on my way downtown. This is how I met Ken, a man who pulls around a two-wheeled cart and collects cans and bottles every day. He also has wavy hair, big blue bedroom eyes, and lashes so long and curly they would make any woman envious. There is a woman bicycle rider who wears a helmet and also collects cans and bottles, and an elderly lady who walks her dogs through the alley every day. They are neighbors whose names I don't always know, but neighbors nonetheless.

Engine Place

As we leave the bougainvillea vine we pass a small gray building that has a floor filled with recycled engines. These shrouded little humps remind me of babies waiting to be born or innocents patiently waiting to pass over to the other side. Though I am sure the owners of this business never view their merchandise this way, it is important to remember Ventura is a mystical place and we all see the world through the perception of our own imaginations.

There are four eating establishments in the first block. The atmosphere in each is unique.

Art's Corner Café

Art's is a clean, sunny place where the service is pleasant, the menu varied, the prices reasonable, and the food tastes like it's homemade.

Corrales Mexican Food to Go

East of Art's is a popular Mexican Restaurant that greets their customers with a small archway and a patio for outdoor dining. The tables and chairs in front are almost always filled whenever Corrales is open.

Casa De Soria

Across the parking lot is Casa De Soria. Its brochure claims it to be the best authentic Mexican food north of the border. This claim has a great deal of merit. Whenever friends who are long-time residents take me out for Mexican food, they usually choose Casa De Soria.

Tony's Steak and Seafood

At the corner of Anacapa and Thompson is one of the most renowned restaurants in town. Ask Venturans who have lived here for any length of time if they know where Tony's is, and they usually do. A visit explains why.

It is rather dark when you go inside. The bar is located in the front of the building, a nice place for a tryst or quiet conversation. The restaurant is cozy and the food and service excellent. Sometimes on the weekends Tony has live entertainment, making it a pleasant place to take a friend, a date, or a spouse for a special night out.

Vehicles Galore

There are so many new and used car dealerships and related businesses along this short stretch of Thompson it is best to put them all together. We skipped over the first one when we went from Casa De Soria to Tony's.

Barber Isuzu

In this block between Santa Cruz and Anacapa, we arrive at one of the many automobile dealerships in town. The place immediately made its presence known to me—and to neighbors for blocks around—by an amplified bell used to announce to employees outside that someone was wanted on the phone in the office.

A friend who had purchased a new Thunderbird often stopped in to visit with me whenever he took his car there to be detailed. Both the automobile and man are now history, and so is the bell. Though I liked the merry jangle because I thought it added to the "color" of the neighborhood, others found it intrusive and silenced it by complaining.

Barber Ford Transportation

This affiliate of Isuzu is four blocks away at the corner of Thompson and Coronado. What it's doing way over there is anyone's guess. Like the lost alleys we have recently visited, it seems to have gone astray.

Enterprise Used Car Sales

This used car lot, located at the southeast corner of Thompson and Santa Cruz, is across the street from Isuzu. The side facing Thompson is an up-front business; the back part, on Prince Alley, reminds me of the rear door in Dr. Jekyll's abode where shadowy figures engaged in furtive activities with Mr. Hyde.

These nighttime visitors chose this spot because tall trees and a big dumpster shield them from the neighbors. Mornings when I walk by and see empty beer cans, cigarette butts, discarded condoms, and other relics of their revelry, I can't help wondering what else has gone on there in the dark hours.

Our next stop it at one of the most enchanting businesses in town.

Ideal Sunroof & Soda

Next door to Enterprise is a business that specializes in T-tops and sunroofs and recycled Coca-Cola vending machines. Glen, the owner, offers a wide variety, unique reminders of the days when you could buy a bottle of pop for a nickel. This place is fun to visit even if you don't need any of the items he sells.

Behind the building, in Prince Alley, is a tall chain link fence that once had a large metal picture of a man and woman wearing old-fashioned swimming suits hooked onto it. These garments cover the human body so completely that if the wearers ventured into water more than four feet deep they could easily drown.

The painting is such a treat. The man, who has black hair parted in the middle and a black mustache, is bare-foot and wearing a red and white striped outfit that looks like long underwear. The woman is decked out in a blue dress and black stockings and has her yellow hair tied up in a scarf.

This picture has vanished only to show up in another place. I liked it so much Glen gave it to me. After repainting it, the "HIDDEN HILLS SWIMMING CLUB" now adorns the south wall of my apartment building where more people can enjoy it than when it was tucked away in the alley.

The following vehicle businesses are listed together.

Premium Pre-Owned Cars and RV's

Next door to Solaris Liquors at the corner of Catalina and Thompson is a car lot with the euphemism "pre-owned." Sounds nicer than "used," doesn't it?

Excellent Deal Auto Sales

This dealership cattycornered from Premium, and others in this area, are a reminder human beings are not the only ones who have had several lifetimes. Vehicles have them, too. A mechanic friend suggested what to watch for when buying a car that has gone through several "incarnations."

The asking price is just a place to start, not what the dealer expects to get. Open the hood and look inside even if you don't know anything about the innards of a car. Then smell it. If it smells bad, don't buy it. Find out the name of the former owner. If the salesman won't give it to you, chances are it was purchased at an auction or something is seriously wrong with it. The most important advice to remember before buying any previously owned vehicle is to make sure it has come from a good home.

The Auto Scrubber

Nestled comfortably amongst all these new and used vehicle lots is a car wash with the logo "Be Kind to Your Car." Next door to the Auto Scrubber is a business with a different focus.

Hertz

This rental agency is housed in a classy gray building beside a parking lot full of modern automobiles. Whenever I see one of these places I am reminded of a trip I took to Seattle several years ago with my daughter Vivian.

We rented a car and were shortly pulled over by a police officer who told us our tags were outdated. I thought it was funny, but

Viv was angry. "The rental agency knows the cops won't give us a ticket because we're from out of town."

But it isn't fair to judge one agency by another, and it didn't seem like something merchants in Ventura would do anyway. One foggy morning I walked by the Hertz place and checked the tags and found all of them were up-to-date.

Kenton Auto Insurance

At the corner of Thompson and Catalina, this insurance company sells inexpensive auto insurance. *Se Habla Espanol.*

Cellular Phones and Pagers

Everyone seems to be buying cellulars now so it is no wonder a place where you can get them is part of the neighborhood. I like this store because it has an inflatable phone that stands before it during business hours, towering as high as the building.

The Prince Alley side, like many of the sites along here, is quite different.

A family has nested here for years in a small motor home with very little yard. Their activities were concealed by large pieces of blue plastic fastened to the chain link fence bordering the property. Occasionally different faces or vehicles appeared and the number of people coming and going varied.

Once in a while I would hear Spanish music or see youngsters playing in the alley. They were good neighbors. They kept to themselves. They are gone now, who knows where? What will happen to the hideaway they occupied? There is no way to tell.

The Door

I reside in a half-block-long building at the corner of Anacapa Street and Thompson Boulevard that contains both businesses and living quarters. The space at the front was rented to a church called The Door. On Sunday mornings and evenings and Wednesday nights, when their religious services took place, music wafted through the walls into the surrounding apartments. It seemed weird because it is not the kind of music you would hear in more conventional churches; it sounded more like jazz or pop music.

I feel the shifting sands of time beneath my pen because The Door has vanished, replaced by musicians who use the space as a recording studio. I can't help wondering how many more of the city's nooks and crannies will disappear before the book is published.

Helen's Light House

Helen's Tarot Card Reading business can be found at the corner of Prince Alley and Anacapa. Questions about her work result in surprising answers.

"I can usually help those who sincerely want information. Many people already know the answer to their questions but are seeking confirmation or to be assured they are wrong.

"Most of my clients want to know about their love lives; a few have unusual concerns. Two wanted to know what happened to deceased relatives. A young woman was worried about her grandmother. (The cards indicated the grandmother worried about her.) Another asked if her late husband ever thought of her. (It didn't look like it.)

"Some of my most frustrating readings have been for a woman who is so angry about things that happened in a past life she can't get on with this one. It's a shame, too, because she's beautiful, smart and talented.

"Another, who was trying to make enough money to get by doing heavy, blue collar work for minimum wage, was looking for a Prince Charming to carry her away to his castle. The cards told a different tale—she could make as much money as she needed but she would have to take a job she didn't like. It was then she admitted that when she was younger she had worked for years in a whorehouse near Las Vegas, sometimes making as much as $8,000 a month.

"When asked what happened to the money she said two husbands, one of whom she had met in the houses, had spent it on their own excesses, leaving her broke and with a child to support. And one had been rotten enough to tell her family the kind of work she did, so they had disowned her.

"If I always told people what they wanted to hear," Helen continued, "I'm sure I'd be rich. But it isn't right. Only charlatans do that."

Do the neighbors ever object to her presence? Helen said she had never had any trouble. "I think they feel safer with me here, as if I'm a good omen or beneficial source of energy."

Since moving into this apartment I have had the feeling many of the people I interact with are people I have known before, perhaps in another lifetime. So I asked Helen about reincarnation and got some interesting answers.

"Many of those we interact with in this lifetime are souls we had unfinished business with in other incarnations. For example, in one of my past lives my older daughter was my father, the younger one a mother who loved me.

"In another regression I saw clearly a female with dark black hair and very white skin who was an enemy disguised as a friend. I recognized her immediately as a woman I had thought was my best friend in this lifetime. But she betrayed me and sabotaged my marriage by having an affair with my husband."

There is a continual change of neighbors in the building as they move in and out. Most of them fall on hard times and can't pay the rent. A recently divorced man was evicted when the landlady caught him raising kittens in his bathroom.

One girl snuck her boyfriend in to live with her, and another was invited to leave because she screamed obscenities out the window all the time.

We had Jed for a while, a nice young man who was always offering to help us single women do things that needed muscle. He left to attend college in L.A.

My favorite actor in this cast of characters is Jim a.k.a. Animal, a talented harmonica player who lives downstairs. His apartment is clean and tastefully decorated in a black, gray, and white décor.

He is a wannabe barber who has worked as a roughneck on the oil platforms for years. One day when I needed to have my hair trimmed and didn't have time to go to the beauty salon I asked if Animal would oblige me. Sure.

"You're letting Animal cut your hair?" a goggle-eyed neighbor asked. Why not? He did a good job.

Sometimes he and his musician friends make a lot of racket, so we have a deal. I'll put up with his noise if he'll put up with mine. Since I have a bad habit of waking during the night with an insatiable urge to pound nails in walls and move pictures, he may be getting the worst of the deal.

Upstairs

The apartment upstairs is one of those places you have to know about or will rarely find. Originally the landlady's boudoir, it commands a view of the southern end of Anacapa Street. If there were no trees the ocean would be visible. Trains rumble through on the tracks the trees hide. Neighbors keep their yards clean and, in one case, filled with flowers.

You have to enter through a gate at the back and cross a shady patio that has a tiny but magical garden that won third place in a national contest sponsored by *New Worlds of Mind and Spirit* magazine. Some nights, according to the woman who lives here, you can see elves and fairies dancing amongst the blossoms. Are these fantasy creatures the result of her vivid imagination? Perhaps, but remember, this is Ventura where spirits, phantoms, and ghosts abound. After you walk up the steep flight of stairs and enter the apartment you will see a delightful studio with an old-fashioned wood-burning fireplace in the corner.

The bathtub in the bathroom is one of those teacup affairs that a person of any size would have trouble fitting into. But the present tenant claims she loves living here because it is filled with nooks and crannies.

She is always finding new hiding places. The attic opens up through a door in an alcove near her desk. There's a small space behind some shelves where she can hide valuables and another above a bookshelf that is difficult to find.

What she likes best is the large open space because she entertains frequently. Unfettered by walls, this apartment has more room for tables and guests than most large homes.

The inland mountains are visible from the east window. Two trees stand atop one of them. Those who have lived here a long time refer to them as "five trees" because that is how many were planted at the turn of the century. Over the years the number has fallen to two. Old-timers in Ventura, a conservative lot, prefer the original name.

Two trees or five, in the days when I regularly sailed to the Channel Islands, they were a welcome sight after a rough crossing.

The Empty House

Across Prince Alley from Helen's Light House is a house that was formerly inhabited by a man and his wife and their two attractive teenage daughters. I used to worry about those kids because word spread around the neighborhood that the parents were dealing drugs. It may have been unfounded gossip, but since the father had not been gainfully employed for four years, the stories were believable.

When they moved they left trash that stretched the entire length of their driveway, was four feet wide and two feet deep. They also abandoned two small dogs. I saw them roaming the neighborhood, frightened orphans.

The house has since been sold to a nice young couple who have a little boy.

The Children

Directly across the alley from the Ideal Sunroof & Soda is an area that has fireplace logs laying about amongst the weeds. At one time you would see a young father cutting them up for firewood to sell to people, a second job to help him support his family.

As he worked five children played nearby, four boys and a little girl. The tale I heard was that the mother, a drug addict, abandoned the family and ran away with her dealer.

These children seem happy and look well cared for. The same is not true of the older "children" who roam the area.

Thompson Boulevard's Hookers

Why prostitutes have chosen this part of the city to ply their trade is not clear. We seem to have as many police vehicles

88 • Ventura: Mystic City by the Sea

patrolling the area as anywhere else. The women are typically young, in their late teens or early twenties, easy to spot because they walk about with vacant eyes and fail to respond to my greetings. Others ask for money, claiming it is to buy food, but more likely to buy drugs or alcohol.

Where are their parents? Why are they on the streets? Child abuse studies reveal at least a third of all the girls who turn to prostitution were incest victims.

Other lost souls who move listlessly about are residents of a nearby shelter for the mentally challenged. One man walks aimlessly, carrying a teddy bear. He could be a danger to himself and others. On at least two occasions residents have been hit by automobiles as they jaywalked across the street.

Since so many of our mental hospitals have been closed it is difficult to know what to do with these adults who will never be more than children. Unfortunately, many of them end up in prison. One hapless fellow had been shooting cattle, imagining himself a big game hunter. Ranchers will hang a man for killing cows in the wild west quicker than they will hang him for killing a person.

He was incarcerated again and again, but whether he was placed in a prison or mental hospital, he always managed so well he was soon released. He coped the best he could with his limited mental abilities until he again did something else to give society another reason to confine him. Is his case unique? Probably not.

MPI Computers

It happened again. Just as I am ready to include a place in this book it disappears. This computer store which was located at the corner of Thompson Boulevard and Anacapa Street is gone. They haven't quit business, just moved away to a new location on Telephone Road. This was despite the friendly influence of the squaw who guarded the doorway warding off evil spirits.

Don, the owner of MPI, and his *compadre,* Debi, guided me

through my first nightmarish days of owning a new computer. I bought it from them on condition they rush to my aid whenever I yelled for help. Good as their word, when these two were busy they once sent Don's teenage son to rescue me.

They seem to enjoy my cyberspace naivete. Don assured me he will continue to be there for me when I need him, and since moving away, he has kept his promise.

Pawn Shop of Ventura

The bright green paint on the front signals the presence of a pawn shop in the same building where the computer business was located. I ventured into the quiet interior to see the owner's extensive collection of pedal cars.

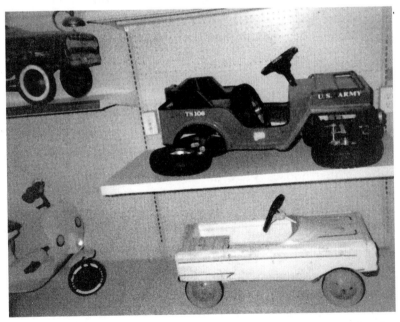

There is a miniature yellow push cart with a fringed top that has Gym-Dandy Surrey written on the side. A police vehicle has hard tires, no top, and a fancy hood ornament. It also has running boards and a string that goes through the steering wheel that's attached to a bell on the front.

The police car reminds me of a dilapidated Model T Ford Dad  owned in the thirties that he used to haul supplies for his paint and wallpaper business. We called it "oogie" because when you wanted to honk at someone you pressed one of the wires protruding from the center of the steering wheel against the metal part and it went "oogie!" It's a wonder we didn't electrocute ourselves.

The Geyser

A spectacular event took place one night at the corner by the pawn shop when the quiet was shattered by the sound of screeching tires and a loud crash. Running to a window I saw one car stopped across the street headed south on the wrong side and another headed in the same direction, on the sidewalk near the wall. The fire hydrant had been snapped off and water shot two stories into the air.

One of the reasons I like living here is because there's always something exciting going on.

Vic's Plumbing Supply and Hurst Furniture

Just east of Tony's Steak and Seafood Restaurant is a long building that houses Vic's plumbing Supply and Hurst Furniture, though the latter is nowhere near Hurst Avenue. There was formerly a small craft shop tucked in between these businesses, but it has gone to join the First Sunday in the Park and the trimmed bougainvillea vines.

I never got around to visiting the little craft store. I regret it now. Perhaps if the neighbors had given them more business they would still be around.

Illusions

This one-story structure at the corner of Thompson and Catalina houses two businesses. The first is a salon called Illusions. You can have your hair, nails, and skin taken care of here, the last includes tanning. Upon entering you find all the woman working there are busy, the ambience friendly.

Kenton Auto Insurance, the company that sells inexpensive automobile insurance, is right next door.

The Rose Garden

Directly behind the pawnshop, on Prince Alley and Anacapa, is a residence occupied by people who love to grow roses. What a treat to gaze from my windows every day and enjoy them without having to take care of them.

Anonymous Neighbors

Many neighbors I know only casually. There are the people who run Hungry Howie's, and Bill. He drives by every day in his small red car on his way to the post office where he has worked "forever." A cheerful woman who lives one house away waves at me whenever she sees me, as do most of the people who travel through Prince Alley on their way to the houses and businesses bordering it.

Since I fit in here so well, I wonder if I haven't met them before in a previous lifetime.

Solaris Liquors

Next door to the pawn shop is a liquor store that opens at 7 a.m. every day except Sunday, when it opens at 8 a.m. It stays open until midnight, except Friday and Saturday, when it doesn't close until 1 a.m. It's nice to know the employees keep such long hours because there are times when I can't sleep or get restless and need someone to talk to.

The place projects a wild kind of energy, not only because they sell spirits but also because of what is for sale on the six news stands in front. Four of them display publications like *The Sun* which features alternative lifestyles want ads: "Hot! Sheet, Hot Lips, Wild Gals for girls, guys and couples." Others are *LAX*

Press and *Dating L.A.* which they claim is "California's largest weekly singles' publication." Off to the side are two newsstands where you can buy the *Los Angeles Times* and the *Ventura County Star* for 25 cents Monday through Saturday, $1.50 on Sunday.

The Viking Motel

This good chi place holds happy memories. Last fall when my brother Dick and sister Jane came to visit, I got them a room at the Viking. Though I made the reservations weeks ahead, they were hard to come by because the place is clean, has kitchens in every unit, and reasonable prices, so people often stay a long time. At the front is a statue of the Virgin Mary which is lighted at night.

Ideal Upholstery

Sometimes things happen that cause energy to be reversed. Negative vibes turn into positive ones, as it did here.

I had passed by this place often when it was Mike's Upholstery but never went in because I hadn't needed their services. Gazing through the front windows I saw some elegantly re-upholstered pieces of furniture. The outside was a different story. An aura of neglect hung about the place. A notice in the front window had more glue on it than letters. One lighted sign said "Open" while two printed ones said "Closed." The front yard was filled with weeds and trash.

Recently the place has been fixed up. The windows are clean and the weeds are gone. A feeling prevails that something nice has happened.

Eric's Tackle Shop

The paintings on the outside of this building are delightful. The door at the west end has a Jaws type shark on it. Teeth bared, it swims directly toward you. Next you see three men on a power boat named the Catherine F. who think they have hooked a big one. But the mermaid below has them fooled. She has seaweed hair, the same color as her tail and, unlike the mermaids of sailors' fantasies, this one is wearing a bra. She has the line in her hands, the hook at the bottom firmly attached to the anchor. Fish of various shapes and sizes and at least one shark swim or fly around, enjoying the spectacle.

Whether the mermaid is trying to help the fishermen by freeing the line or is just messing with them by jerking on it is difficult to tell. But she is smiling so mischievously, I suspect the latter. Around the corner of the building a huge marlin leaps above the waves, leading the fishermen to believe that is what they've caught.

The most intriguing thing about this mural is the very different faces on everyone. I speculate the artist, whose name is Prosser, knows the characters involved—the mermaid as a human nymph—and has captured their likenesses accurately.

The next five shops are all at the front of the San Clemente Apartment Building. As I walk by and pick up the vibrations radiating out it reminds me of a tiny, self-contained community where the residents get along well and watch out for their neighbors.

Diamond Communications
The popularity of air touch cellular phones is the reason so many of these places are able to stay in business.

Labor Ready
Every morning, except Sundays and holidays, I see men standing outside waiting for work. So far I have seen only one woman.

I had contacted them when getting bids on putting a new gate in the wall of my patio and was favorably impressed. They got back to me quickly with an estimate that seemed fair and included the permits and other items needed.

The Video Aid Station

This little shop with the creative name has a sign on the door that says *The best in satellite TV system sales and installations. Serving Ventura County since 1987.*

The Kayak Shop

Until a friend mentioned kayaking around Ventura Harbor I had never considered it a sport for middle-aged or elderly women. My introduction to this shop had nothing to do with kayaks. One day, when I turned from Prince Alley onto San Clemente, I blew out a tire. The proprietor, Travis Perch, who lives in an apartment above his business, heard the bang and came downstairs and changed it for me.

The Grocery Store

At the corner of San Clemente and Thompson is the Carniceria Guadalajara grocery store. Next to the word "Guadalajara" is the picture of a raging bull.

I am fond of this grocery, not only because it has a fresh meat counter and is two blocks from where I live, but because the people who work here take good care of their customers. I have seen the cashier open a new pack and sell a fellow who was desperate for a cigarette just *one*, which was all he could afford.

This is a family run operation where pre-school brown-eyed children play about. It is a friendly addition to the neighborhood, a nice change from the huge grocery chains where choices are abundant but the atmosphere commercial.

The San Clemente Apartments

As I walk along Prince Alley I often have a chance to see into some of the units. They look clean and well cared for, the amiable tenants owners of nice cars.

Someday I may live here because I like the area, despite what happened to me a little further down the way.

The Case of the Misguided Landlady

Shades of Perry Mason, but this misadventure describes the experience I had. After deciding to move from The Beachfronter, I cast about for a home or apartment to share and found a space for rent in a house on San Clemente. I was delighted with the location because the street is lined with sheltering trees that offer shade the year around and because it is only a block from the railroad tracks.

I should have paid attention to my intuition because right from the start I had a feeling something was wrong. It seemed perfect with only one other woman, one cat, and an empty ground floor room that included laundry and kitchen privileges. I was anxious to move in because I was going to spend the summer months with a friend on a boat harbored at Catalina.

What the real problem was is a mystery. But no sooner had I gotten everything in, and was sitting, exhausted, on the couch in the apartment I was moving from, than my new landlady called and said she had decided not to rent the room to me after all. The excuse she gave was that I had left cracker crumbs on the floor in the kitchen and neglected to wipe out the sink in the bathroom after using it.

All this seemed incredibly petty coming from a woman who left her kitty litter box in the kitchen right next to the refrigerator, but I wasn't going to argue. It turned out for the best because if she hadn't evicted me I never would have found the apartment on Prince Alley.

My Favorite Watering Hole

At the northeast corner of San Clemente and Thompson is Harris's Puretec Water Pure Express. It is a machine with four stations that dispenses clear, drinkable water for ten cents a gallon.

Remembering the muddy liquid the city worker pulled up from the underground river, I appreciate the opportunity to buy water so inexpensively.

The place is always busy, but what impressed me the most was the visit I had early one morning with a man who was servicing the machine. "I used to think these things were a racket," he admitted. "Not anymore. Mr. Harris doesn't want this water to meet the city's standards; he wants it to be better."

Living in Ventura is akin to living in a flower basket the year round because the blossoms always give off an inviting aroma, like they do at our next stop.

Savannah's Garden

Near the end of Prince Alley is a tiny flower stand, one of many in the city. Savannah's Garden is open Monday, Wednesday and Friday from 12 to 6. I admire those who are enterprising enough to run businesses like this. I envision them as people who moonlight to help support their families or better their lot in life.

Abednego Book Shoppe

Across the parking lot from Savannah's is the Abednego Book Shoppe. The sign on the front advertises "Rare, New or Used, Greeting Cards, Book Searches and Collectibles." I have to be careful in book stores because I love them and am always taken in by a wonderland of make-believe. I see books my girls or friends would like, so lose my head and impulsively buy more than I intended.

This bookstore hasn't been here very long. I hope they are successful for they are a welcome addition to the neighborhood.

Ventura Trophy Company

Competition breeds a fierce kind of energy that is exemplified by getting trophies. Whenever I drive by this place I remember something that happened at one of our bridge sectionals because the trophies awarded to the winners were purchased here.

The tournament attracts players from all over the country, some of them less than honorable. Leaving the trophies on the directors' table, the tournament director assumed they would be safe because the hall where the games are held is locked at night.

The next day, to the director's dismay, he discovered that not only had someone stolen two of the trophies, the thief had taken a huge bouquet of roses and a bowl filled with candy, too.

Having finished this intimate visit with the homes and residences along Prince Alley, I wonder about the other parts of town. What happens there? What are other peoples' stories and experiences? Are they much different? I suspect they are not.

We leave the inland area of the city now and venture forth to the Pacific Ocean. This mighty body of water is the source of much of the Godly energy on the earth, and some of the Devil's own mischief as well.

The following tale, though it can't be blamed directly on the sea, is an example of the mayhem evil forces bring down on ships and sailors at incautious moments.

World's First Oil Tanker Burns and Sinks at Ventura!

On the night of June 25, 1889, the SS Harrison, a 160-foot schooner-rigged steamer, caught fire at the Ventura Wharf and burned all night sending flames and explosions into the sky.

The spectacle was described by John McGonicle of the *Ventura Democrat* as "One of the greatest pictures the eye can look upon." The disaster was publicly blamed on the Chinese cook who was said to have started the fire in the ship's galley. Insurance records indicate the true culprit was a sailor who, when asked to check if the forward bunker was full of oil, had lowered a lit kerosene lantern into the hold. Fortunately, no lives were lost.

CHAPTER SIX

Ventura's Marina and Beaches

We have now arrived at some of San Buenaventura's most mystical sites—her marina and beaches. For mysterious reasons, the marina is a place that's difficult for some people to find. A friend visiting from out of town once asked a mail carrier, a *local* mail carrier, where it was, and was told he didn't know. Why it chooses to remain an enigma is anyone's guess. It may be because haunting spirits abide here in great numbers and don't want unwelcome entities intruding upon their haven.

The Mushroom Farm

Along the way to the marina (which can be reached from the 101 by going south on Telephone Road to Olivas Park Drive) you will pass the mushroom farm. With 370 people working here it is one of Ventura's biggest employers. You can buy mushrooms of all sizes for reasonable prices, especially if you are a senior citizen, but you can't look around. In bygone days they conducted tours, now there is too great a danger of the mushrooms becoming contaminated.

Ventura Isles Marina

After leaving the mushroom plant, go west on Olivas Park Drive, past the Adobe Historical Monument and Olivas Park Golf Course (surely one of the world's most beautiful) to

Harbor Boulevard. After you cross it you will be on Spinnaker Drive and soon afterward at the marina. If you turn the wrong direction, don't worry; Spinnaker ends and you can retrace your steps. But before you do, remember to make an X in the dirt for good luck.

Another way to find this seaside resort is to hop on a jolly little vehicle that, after it meanders around town and near the ocean for a while, will take you right to it.

The Trolley

Once again, just as I am ready to include something in this book, it vanishes. I am beginning to think more than apparitions of humans are the ghosts in this city. The trolley comes and goes, vulnerable to monies available in the city budget.

It is too bad we had to lose this cartoon-like conveyance. Painted bright colors, it scooted along to the Channel Islands National Park Visitor's Center, Main Street at Chestnut, City Hall, Santa Clara, San Buenaventura Mission and the Amtrak stop at Seaside Park. On its way back to Ventura Harbor Village it swung by the California Street Plaza at the Holiday Inn, the Ventura Beach Hotel, formerly the Doubletree, Seaward Village at the Beach, Peninsula Drive at Pierpont Boulevard and the Four Points Sheraton. It left the marina every hour on the hour until 5:00 p.m., Wednesday through Sunday and holiday Mondays. A 45-minute ride cost one dollar.

Mike, the trolley driver who gave me such colorful information about the city the first time, was not the driver on the last day. I missed out on the opportunity to confirm some of the things he had told me. No matter; I trust the city will find the money eventually and put the trolley back into service. Something much worse happened to an earlier conveyance.

In 1893 a small horse-drawn service was begun and the Ventura and Ojai Railway laid tracks down the yet-to-be paved Main Street that extended from the railway station to Ventura Avenue.

In 1908 when the state provided funds for cities to pave their main streets the trolley company opposed the plan, claiming the paving would cover the trolley tracks.

Worried that Ventura would soon be the only city in California with dirt streets, on Halloween a group of pranksters broke into the trolley barn and pushed the trolleys into the ocean. Tracks are still occasionally uncovered when work is done on Main Street.

This story reminds me of a recent incident when a neighbor claimed I had parked so close to his vehicle he couldn't get out, and threatened that if I ever did it again he would tow my car away and dump it in the ocean!

Ventura Harbor Village

My first acquaintance with the marina occurred a few years ago when I visited Helen's Light House. It was located in the Carousel Building and had a view of the harbor and wooden sidewalk in front of the shops.

Helen had to leave when the place acquired a new owner. She didn't vanish but moved to an apartment on Prince Alley where she still does psychic readings with Tarot cards.

The Carousel

The building is now filled with dozens of arcade games, a gift shop and a snack bar. It still has the full-sized 36-horse carousel that is available for parties. This animal merry-go-round is fun to ride whether you are young or just young at heart.

Andria's Seafood Restaurant and Market

There are many restaurants in the marina. Andria's is arguably the most famous, having been voted "best seafood" for 14 years in a row according to the brochure the visitors' information center hands out. As you make your way along Spinnaker you pass docks and boat slips and, just as the marina comes into view, a restaurant known for the fresh fish and camaraderie it dishes out every day.

You can order a small meal à la carte, a piece of freshly fried fish, which always turns out to be two pieces, and a side of salad that doesn't cost much and is just right for a light lunch. The menu is varied, but the staff specializes in seafood harvested from the ocean daily. They also have a fresh fish market at the back of the restaurant. Every weekend from 8 to 11 a.m. a Fishermen's and Farmer's Market is open on Andria's Pier.

You can eat indoors or out and, since they have posted signs that say "Please don't feed the birds," it is safe to sit at sunlit tables and enjoy the food and a spectacular view of a harbor filled with tall ships, fishing boats, and ocean-going yachts.

Hornblower's

Upstairs, across the parking lot from Andria's, is a restaurant that nurtures comedic talent. Every Friday and Saturday night comic wannabe's are invited to appear before the dinner crowd. A banner claims it is the "Original Comedy Club Since 1983" and the marina brochure indicates it has been voted "Best Comedy" for 10 years. Some of the performers are funny and some of them are not. But you have to give this place credit for a unique idea and for giving those with the ability to see the light side of life and a passion to share their talents a place to display them.

Milano's

Downstairs from Hornblower's is Milano's, one of the best Italian restaurants in town. Their cuisine is served up with a million dollar view of the harbor, visible from every table.

Frulatti's

Next door to Milano's, this Italian restaurant enjoys an outdoor patio and the same spectacular view. Like all the businesses that front on the ocean's waves, it pulses with energy.

Ventura Dive & Sport

Where but in a seaside marina could you find a place that teaches people how to scuba dive in the ocean? Dive and Sport has its own heated pool and offers dive trips to the Channel Islands.

While here I am reminded of a story told by my scuba-diving brother, Richard O'Dell. Called upon to retrieve the body of a farmer who had drowned at the base of a dam in a lake in southeastern Colorado, he found the corpse with no trouble. But he was puzzled by the sight of tooth marks, as if something had been biting or chewing on it. The mystery was soon solved by the appearance of a catfish the size of a shark. The monster had grown this huge by feeding upon fish and other "debris" trapped near the dam's intake. Unnerved, Dick "got the hell out of there."

Mike's Marine Classics

If you prefer to stay on top of the water you will be interested in the three vessels belonging to Erik and Lia Sluyter. They have a bunk and breakfast business, an innovative seaside variation of a bed and breakfast.

They offer a Mahalo 43-foot houseboat that sleeps four and has two state rooms, hot running water, shower, dining room, and galley with electric stove, refrigerator, and microwave. The Interlude is a 46-foot power boat that sleeps four and is as comfortable as the Mahalo. Aloha is a 34-foot sailboat that sleeps two and has a cozy sitting area and great cockpit. Also available is a harbor ride on the Bay Queen.

Coastal Cone Company

Rounding the corner onto the wooden boardwalk most summer weekends you will see a long line of people waiting in front of The Coastal Cone Company. This popular spot offers 32 flavors of ice cream and yogurt, and has a full fountain.

High Cees

High Cees is a bar where more than wine and beer and mixed drinks are served up on weekends. As a live band plays, dancers add great excitement in the crowded room as skirts fly toward the ceiling.

Like the other bars and liquor stores around Ventura, it has both dark and light energy. It was closed for a while when a former owner fell from a dock and drowned near a haunted ship.

Duchess III

A few years ago a friend and I attended a lecture about this old vessel given by our local ghost expert Richard Senate and his psychic wife Debbie. The plan was that we would walk around the boat with divining rods made from wire coat hangers and find the "hot spots," places where people had been murdered or fallen overboard.

You programmed the rods by instructing them to tell you "yes" or "no" according to how they moved while you held them loosely in your hands. Gentle readers, if you don't believe in psychic phenomenon, skip this next part.

As I sat there trying to give my divining rods instructions, they took on a life of their own, swaying back and forth across each other. The movement began slowly, then became more vigorous, eventually whacking my shoulders. I understood the message perfectly. I wasn't being reprimanded by someone who had passed over, but by a disgruntled lover who is still alive and very angry with me for leaving him.

Just how I received this information is unexplainable. But I had no doubt then, nor have I since, what the message was and who sent it. He thinks of me often and visits once in a while, not in my dreams, but in visions. Some of you nonbelievers may call these hallucinations or an overactive imagination, but those of us who are psychic know better.

Unfortunately, this magnificent ocean liner has been retired and is no longer available as a setting for Richard's lectures.

Greek at the Harbor

Next door to the High Cees, this restaurant is a treat for anyone with a taste for Greek food and entertainment. In addition to the gourmet fare, they have female belly dancers and male dancers who perform in costume while balancing glasses of water on their heads.

Etc.

As delightful as The Greek is, there are other restaurants and shops that are just as commendable. But it isn't realistic to include all of them within these pages, so I have limited myself to a broad sampling.

The tourist brochure indicates this 33 acres of prime waterfront has 35 specialty shops and restaurants. Parents might be interested in the Kids' Harborland that is open every Wednesday through Saturday from noon to 4 p.m. that has a petting zoo, jolly jump and face painting. Buckaroo pony rides are available every weekend from noon to 5 p.m., weather permitting.

Powerboat owners will like the offshore races. Those who prefer less competitive water activities can enjoy narrated cruises, or kayak, pedal, and electric boat rentals. Shoppers can browse through the fresh seafood market. The Harbor Hatter, with over 1000 styles in stock has the greatest selection on the West Coast. The Glass Touch features collectibles, Tiffany lamps, and crystals. And don't miss Harbor Books.

If you purchase the Feng Shui book at Oriental Treasures, Ltd., you will discover you are going to need lots of crystals to get rid of the negative chi (energy) in your home or office!

Some people will be interested in learning what happened to a couple who was having financial trouble. One of the suggestions in the book is to keep the lid on the toilet closed so there is no hole for the money to slip through.

"What the heck," her husband said, when his wife suggested it. "Couldn't hurt anything."

Though they took it as a joke, magical things happened. First, she received a $5,000 refund from her insurance carrier because she had been paying too much for some prescription medicine for years. Then the mosaics she creates began to sell. Next, the husband, who was in real estate but collected no commissions in months, suddenly had three houses in escrow.

Skeptics will claim these things would have happened anyway. Those who have experienced the power of chi know better.

The County and Coast Reporter

Upstairs, in the building across from the carousel, is a newspaper office. *The County and Coast Reporter* is a great read because it tells about interesting people and events that take place around the city's harbors and beaches, and because it's free!

Parade of Lights

Once every year, on the first weekend in December, Ventura Harbor hosts an event in which boat owners decorate their vessels in the theme chosen for that year and parade them at night before admiring spectators. This is a beautiful not-to-be missed experience that is unique to cities fortunate enough to enjoy harbors and a warm climate the year around. If you are in the area this time of the year, treat yourself and your friends and loved ones to this fairy tale parade.

Before you leave the marina go see the museum.

Channel Islands National Park Visitor's Center

At the end of Spinnaker Drive you will find a museum in the same building as the Visitor's Information Booth. Here you can learn about the park through programs by rangers, exhibits, a living tide pool, and movies. Occasionally the staff members display paintings by Robert Wassell who specializes in seascapes of the Channel Islands.

Fascinating to me were models of the islands, those mighty lumps of land guarding the entrance to Ventura's harbors and beaches. We will visit them soon, but first, let's check out our world famous beaches.

It is important to keep in mind these are not just long stretches of sand with a huge body of water nearby, but mystical places. They exert a life force that nourishes our souls and draws the water people of the world inexorably to them.

McGrath State Beach

This beach just south of Ventura's city limits has well maintained campgrounds with a spectacular view. Those who are partial to this kind of leisurely, family-oriented activity, will enjoy the facilities and the sand and surf.

South Jetty Beach

Bordering Spinnaker Drive at the entrance to Ventura Harbor is a swimming beach. Guarded by a breakwater at the harbor's entrance, this protected area affords swimmers a safe place to play in sight of sailboats, dolphins, and other marine life.

Longboard's Grill

Before continuing up the coastline we will visit the Longboard Grill across the harbor on Anchors Way near the Harbor Master's office. Their yellow pages ad says, "The best sunsets, patio dining, fresh fish, pizzas, salads, sandwiches, seafood, exotic drinks, steaks, oysters, shrimp."

The surfboard and seaside decorations inside are as enjoyable as the view.

Ventura Beach

This narrow strip of sand stretches from the north edge of

Ventura Harbor to the Ventura River. It begins at Marina Park and can be reached only by boat or by driving to the end of Pierpont Boulevard. It is another family-friendly recreational site with a north jetty that pokes out into the ocean and ends near the breakwater.

Seaward Avenue

Continuing on past beach shanties and mansions we come to my favorite street in town. This two-block-long strip of Seaward on the ocean side of Highway 101 houses Joannafina's. They had a booth at the Fourth of July Fair where I bought homemade tortillas.

Here too is Duke's, famous for succulent hamburgers and an informality that encourages diners to throw their peanut shells on the straw-covered floor. If you prefer, you can sit outside at a bar or one of the tables and people-watch.

The Inn at the Beach is located at the water's edge. A friend who lives in Illinois stays here every chance she gets, claiming it has one of the most beautiful views on earth.

The Brothel isn't there anymore—another ghost that has disappeared. But once upon a time, in the building where Eric Erickson's Restaurant was located, it existed. This part of the tale is true; another story I heard probably isn't.

Mike, the trolley driver, told me there was a gang of bikers, not members of Hell's Angels, who hung out near the Brothel. The most famous, he said, was Ace Venturi who is now the governor of Minnesota.

I wrote the governor, whose name is Jess Ventura, and asked him about it but never heard back. This may be because I am not eligible to vote in that state or because Ventura thought the question too laughable to warrant a response.

Ami, who lived in that neighborhood for 30 years, said she never heard of a motorcycle gang around there, so I believe

Mike may have gotten his story mixed up with a movie or TV program in which the main character was named Ace Venturi. The governor, a former wrestler, is rumored to have adopted the name, Ventura, not because he had ever lived here, but because he liked it.

Mike also said there was a silver-haired attorney who drove a silver colored pickup who could tell me about it. But I have been unable to locate the man. None of the other old timers I talked to in town knew about him, or the motorcycle gang, either. So once again have I found a myth, a man, or just heard a fable?

The Hungry Hunter

This extraordinary restaurant's literature says, "For those who enjoy early dining we offer the following entrees at a special price. Ask your food server for details. All entrees are served as a complete meal."

Recently I heard the discount meals were no longer available. It doesn't matter for, prices aside, the Hungry Hunter is a great place to dine.

A Simple Recipe

One item on the Hungry Hunter's menu, their Beer Batter Shrimp entrée, reminds me of an easy but delicious recipe. You combine equal parts beer and flour and let the batter set three hours. The beer breaks down the gluten in the flour and makes it light, wonderful as a coating for fried onion rings. Since my culinary expertise is much like playing Russian Roulette with food, two or three item recipes are favorites.

The Lifeguard Station

This newly constructed building, located between Seaward Avenue and the Ventura Pier, shelters those responsible for the safety of swimmers in the turbulent Pacific. Occasionally signs are posted warning people to stay out of the water because of the dangerous undertow. The station has wheelchairs available with tires that are wide enough to ride across the sand.

Ventura Pier

Great sailing vessels once docked alongside this lengthy pier, known forever to old timers as the Wharf. The water is so shallow now it is difficult to imagine ships of any size docking there.

For years the far end of the pier was fenced off, declared unsafe. Later, at great cost to taxpayers, it was rebuilt with a fountain at its end that spouted water as the tide surged. Unfortunately, the rebuilt portion washed away again; the ocean thwarting mankind's best efforts at reconstruction. This was a loss not only for sightseers and the children and adults who loved the fountain many called the whale, but for fishermen as well.

We humans often underestimate the water's power. If the sea doesn't want the pier entrenching upon it that far, the pier is not going to survive.

At the beach end of the pier you will find the new Erik Erickson's Restaurant. Swallows on their way to Capistrano can be seen from here in the fall when they fly south to avoid cold weather.

Promenade Park

The walkway begins at the end of San Pedro Street and runs along the ocean's edge between the 101 and Harbor Boulevard. It continues under the pier and beside the Holiday Inn, some seaside condominiums, and an apartment house. Then it curves up alongside the Ventura River, across the railroad tracks to where the bicycle path between Ventura and Ojai join. On the map it looks like the Promenade runs from the mall just east of the Holiday Inn and Figueroa.

It is well-traveled by men, women, children, bike riders, those on roller blades and peddle carts and others enjoying the sun and sights. One of the bicycle riders is man who likes to dress in costumes. On the Fourth of July he is Uncle Sam; at Christmastime, Santa Claus. Rumor has it he is an old fellow who often wears top hat and tails, and collects aluminum cans.

Another biker, jealously guarding his Honda, took it with him into the Holiday Inn's restroom. How he got so mixed up that he went in the Ladies' Room instead of the Men's is unknown. He certainly unnerved a couple of women who found him there.

Most of those on the promenade walk. It is a pleasant place to stroll and as safe as anywhere else in town—except at night. The positive chi deserts this beach after dark, making it dangerous for those who trespass.

Like other cities of any size, there are spots where troublemakers hang out, and this is one of them. After sundown they don't want anyone interfering with their nefarious activities.

Surfer's Point

The largest Chumash settlement in Ventura, called Shishalop, was located near Surfer's Point. Settled in 1000 A.D. it was last mentioned in mission records in 1805.

Recently, dozens of rock sculptures were created at Surfer's Point by Stuart Finch, a homeless man passing through, to "make people smile."

This strip of sand is where surfer's gather to enjoy a sport that is available to young and old, male and female. While I was living at the Beachfronter I could see little dark spots in the water often before the sun rose, heads of surfers waiting for enough light to catch a wave.

The Sighting

One afternoon, near the Ventura River Estuary where a neighbor and I were walking, we saw something exciting. Behind us swimmers and surfers frolicked in the gentle waves. To our left five huge inhabitants of the ocean appeared, swimming sedately, all in a row, headed north to cooler waters.

I don't whether they were dolphins, whales, or sharks, but they all had fins and they were huge. As there was no panic along the shoreline, I assumed they were dolphins. But since they weren't playing and jumping about, I may be mistaken. Regardless, they were a breathtaking sight I will never forget; one of the things that makes living near the sea so exciting.

California Beach Party

The first year I lived in Ventura the city's annual Beach Party was an unfenced festival on the promenade. Decorated with yellow, orange, and hot pink streamers on tall poles, it attracted families and tourists, and rabble rousers. The city had so much trouble they had to fence the area off and charge admission to pay for the security guards. Eventually the event was turned over to private enterprise.

The last time I attended the Beach Party it was half as big and not nearly as much fun. Even worse, the colorful banners and streamers were gone. It may become a thing of the past, done in by those whose dark ids spoil things for everyone.

Beachfronter Apartments

The first time I saw this place I was spellbound and wouldn't be contented until I found a way to live there. An upstairs apartment in the 200 building was my home the first five years I resided in Ventura. The Beachfronter is the only seaside apartment complex between San Francisco and San Diego that has no power lines or roads between it and the water. Comprised of single and double bedroom units, it is one of the most desirable rental locations in the state.

The Fairgrounds with its plethora of activities and the Derby Club are a coconut's throw to the west; a condominium complex with an ocean view directly east. Separating these buildings is a block-long street named Paseo de Playa. Accessible only from Harbor Boulevard, it affords public parking to the hordes of men and women who throng to the beach when the "Surf's up!" cry reverberates throughout the town.

Anyone who loves trains will be especially happy at the Beachfronter. Amtrak zips through several times a day, stopping at a station just a few steps west at the end of Harbor Boulevard. In the early hours of the morning freight trains rumble by. (A man whose father who worked for a rail line for many years claims the number of freighters predicts times of prosperity or recession more accurately than the pundits on Wall Street.)

Though these recently redecorated units are charming and beautifully landscaped, the location is their greatest asset. By day the ocean laps the shoreline, delighting those who play upon the promenade. By night the same waves lull residents to sleep.

Within easy walking distance are the conveniences of Main Street and Thompson Boulevard. The post office is a short stroll away, as is the Saturday Farmer's Market. One of the city's most scenic off-ramps rises from the intersection at Harbor and California, giving those who traverse it a breathtaking view of the Pacific Ocean and, in the distance, visible from that stretch of the 101, Hollywood Beach. But the Beachfronter has some little goblins cavorting about. At least it did when I lived there.

Sharing an apartment with a roommate means you do as many things as possible outside the only bathroom. For this reason I always sat at my dresser to set my hair. I dampened it with water and when finished, dumped the remaining liquid out the window. No problem as there was nothing down there except shrubbery—most of the time.

One day I received an irate phone call from the manager asking if I had thrown something out the kitchen window a few minutes earlier. "No, I tossed some water out my bedroom window. Why?"

The maintenance man, quietly working below, got soaked, but let out not a peep. He stalked home to shower and put on dry clothes, convinced someone had a grudge against him. Poor guy. It wasn't funny since he quit soon afterward. But I have a hard time not laughing whenever I think about it.

Tortilla Flats

Before the city turned the area just beyond Figueroa into the fairgrounds, it was known as Tortilla Flats, home to many low income residents like the family of Ken, the can man. "People there took care of each other," he explained. "Sure, we were poor, but there wasn't much crime."

Though there is a campaign underway to keep the colorful murals that grace the entrance where they are, they may be moved to Ventura Avenue. When the 101 was built Tortilla Flats vanished and became the fairgrounds, location of many of the city's commercial events.

Improvements are made from time to time. Not too many years ago the Promenade was extended past Figueroa. Even before construction began I heard part of the new path would be washed away by the ocean, and it happened. A portion of it is fenced off now, unsafe for pedestrian or other traffic.

Sometimes it seems in our zeal to protect the fragile life along our shorelines projects are undertaken that don't make sense. The extension of the promenade is one of them. There must be a practical way to protect the interests of both residents of the ocean and those who walk upon the land and pay taxes.

As mentioned earlier, when telling of the pier being destroyed, you can't mess around with the ocean. Never mind that "Pacific" means peaceful. If that body of water doesn't want a walkway there, it's going to find a way to get rid of it.

Seaside Park

Seaside Park is often referred to as "Hobo Jungle." Long ago it was a place where vagrants camped while waiting for trains to slow down to cross the bridge so the men could hop on a freight car and ride to their next destination.

There is still always something going on; nowhere else is this old city filled with so much energy. Saturday nights are enlivened by the roar of the stock car races. Beachfronter residents recall times when the Grateful Dead rock group had a concert at the park and deadhead groupies used the fountains and swimming pool as bathtubs.

The park's brochure lists events such as horse shows including team roping, equestrian, and cross country. Other shows include home and garden, classic cars, guns, Southwest Indian art, computers, exotic birds, horses, rabbits, Beanie Babies, cats, all-breed dogs, antiques, trains, and oldies. There are flea markets galore, swap meets for motorcycles, and fairs—the biggest one is the Ventura County Fair.

Ventura County Fair

Once a year in August, Seaside Park hosts the county fair. It is a popular event, great fun for young and old alike. In the past it was a holiday for three cultures.

Chumash People held ritual dances and erected decorated poles and flew banners made of colorful feathers; the Spanish and Mexican peoples held religious processions, bull fights and fiestas; the Yankees entertained themselves with horse races and a fair.

This year one of the main attractions was guys on fake horses that made them look like they were riding the horses. The "cowboys" walked around wearing long blankets and saddles with false legs hanging over the sides. Children would pet the noses of the "horses" because they seemed so much like real animals when the men galloped about.

The most popular exhibit was the sow who had just given birth to a litter of piglets. As she lay on her side sleeping, they would squeal and holler, trying to get to her teats to have their dinner.

Never do I miss the fudge concession. I enjoy watching them knead the sugary mass, wondering how they avoid spilling it over the side of the table.

The Derby Club

Their brochure claims: "You're a winner at the Derby Club!"

This off-track betting facility has annual memberships, pre-sale admission cards, gift certificates, and the opportunity to hold meetings or other events there. Ever since the Derby Club opened, the fairgrounds have been solvent.

The few times I was in the place I was uncomfortable without knowing why. Perhaps it was because I was married to a man who gambled and all my memories of this form of entertainment are bad. Other people certainly don't have that problem.

One of my Beachfronter roommates, Rich, had chosen the apartment because he frequented the Derby Club. His stories of how red tape kept people from winning made me wonder if the poor fellow's brain was functioning. Though I am sure everything was done legally, he lost so much, like most compulsive gamblers, that he had to move back with his family. It was a shame; he was the best roommate I ever had.

Despite what their brochure claims, I suspect there are very few winners at the Derby Club.

More Beaches

The city limits ends at the edge of Seaside Park, but the beaches don't. Immediately across the Ventura River is the Emma Wood State Beach. Here, as you head north, you see flocks of sea gulls and other exotic birds, endangered species protected in this sanctuary.

Rincon Beach

Not far north of Ventura's city limits, alongside the 101, is a residential area located at the water's edge. The homes are lovely, the area secluded and quite safe. It was not always so. Bayard Taylor, a literary light in California during the Gold Rush of 1849 wrote a poem about the Rincon that describes a great battle that took place on these shores in the early part of the last century.

The Fight of Paseo Del Mar

Gusty and raw was the morning,

A fog hung over the seas,

And its gray skirts rolling inward,

Were torn by the mountain trees.

No sound was heard but the dashing

Of waves on the sandy shore,

When Pablo of San Diego

Rode down to the Paseo Del Mar.

The poem is much longer, but this gives an idea of the battle that ensued.

Carpinteria State Beach

Carpinteria State Beach has campgrounds that are so popular you have to reserve a space months in advance.

A friend was going to take me to the San Miguel Campsite, her favorite, and tell stories about her experiences there. But on the way to my home she had a car accident and couldn't make it. Later she invited me to camp out there with her one night but before we could do it she got sick and had to come home.

Convinced I was bad luck for her, I went alone and found the view magnificent, the other campers friendly and the facilities everything you could desire. The beaches farther up the coast are special, too, one of them for a unique reason.

The Nude Beach

Ever since I began this book I planned to include this secluded spot. The trouble was I couldn't get any of my friends to go with me to investigate. I had been there once with a fellow I was dating, and had been warned we had to be careful because occasionally there were police raids.

That outing was a dismal disappointment, especially for my escort. Despite the fact he had brought a gourmet lunch and a bottle of champagne, I wasn't much fun. I am so miserable in hot sunlight I spent the time huddled beneath a beach towel trying to keep cool. And we didn't get arrested, either.

I had forgotten where the beach was located for it was just a memory, same as the fellow who took me. But if I was going to write about it I had to have some idea where it is located. I cajoled Ami until she finally agreed to go on condition she didn't have to take off her clothes.

She thought it was near Summerland so we started there. Wrong. But a woman who was sunbathing on the beach at Lookout Park while her two German shepherd dogs frolicked in the water suggested we get on the road that ran beside the railroad tracks and head back the way we came.

We drove along Via Real, which parallels the 101, went under an underpass, and finally found the beach we were searching for just west of Loon Point. We found nude sunbathers, too, or would have if the gendarmes hadn't been there. Some influential residents had raised a fuss so the cops were handing out tickets that day. Their M.O. is to post an officer on a nearby cliff, have him spot those who frolic sans clothing and then send others down to hassle them. Though I'm a law-abiding citizen and regrettably don't have a story of being arrested in the nude to pass on to future generations, I think it is too bad people were objecting to the nudists' activities.

Everyone we interviewed, including one grizzled old timer who looked toasty brown all over, claimed he and the other sunbathers never created problems. They may not misbehave but it was pretty obvious they were bothering people who had enough clout to see that something was done. The trip home gave us a clue as to who they were.

Padaro Lane

Padaro Lane parallels the101. As we drove toward Ventura we passed HUGE estates—the kind you see on TV's *Lifestyles of the Rich and Famous*. The magnificently fenced and gated areas outside these places and Beach Club Road indicated the wealth and influence of the people who lived there. The further we drove the smaller the lots became, until we reached the Santa Claus Lane turnoff and got back on the freeway.

I suspect the rich homeowners are the ones who wanted the law enforcement community to "clean up" the beaches. Some time in the future I'll return see how much luck they had.

The suntanned old timer didn't seem too worried. When asked about all the $50 tickets he'd received he said, "They don't bother me none. I just throw 'em away."

Oil Platforms

This book wouldn't be complete without mentioning the oil platforms. I wanted to visit the one my neighbor, Animal, worked on but he said that for security reasons it wouldn't be possible. Instead he showed me a tape a fellow roustabout had made.

Hermosa is 20 miles offshore, a 45-minute helicopter ride from Santa Barbara. A flame burns off excess gas, and the workmen re-drill if production is low. Some women are employed there but it's mostly men. The crew, who is usually out a week at a time, works 12-hour shifts.

The oil platforms will soon be gone. The environmentalists have objected so much the oil companies are in the process of abandoning them. Too bad. Not only are these manmade islands a major source of revenue, they also make us less dependent upon foreign oil. Besides, I find them beautiful. At night they resemble floating Christmas trees. Shining, they send their energy ashore like a blessing.

I saw eternity the other night,

Like a great ring of pure and endless light,

All calm as it was bright.

—Henry Vaughn

Channel Islands

In the warm months these massive chunks of land disappear from-view, lost in the haze. There are seven of them. Starting at the north are San Miguel, then Santa Rosa, Santa Cruz, and Anacapa, the one closest to Ventura.

Farther south is tiny Santa Barbara Island, Santa Catalina, and San Clemente. Most of my sailing expeditions involved Anacapa and Catalina; the latter was where I spent one long, miserable summer.

When I belonged to a single's group called Pacific Currents Sailing Club, we went to Anacapa often. My first trip aboard a small sailing vessel gave me a taste of what to expect in the future. Told we were going to Forney's for lunch, I envisioned a restaurant where I could order a meal. That's not exactly how it was. Forney's is a cove; the lunch was whatever the others and I had brought to share.

I like this organization. It is different from most single's clubs because the members have a common interest—sailing. You didn't have to own a boat to belong, either. Those who do, mostly men, are just glad to have company.

Santa Catalina Island Adventure

It seemed like every time I boarded a sailing vessel I got hurt. The most memorable injury occurred at Catalina Island where a friend and I had gone to spend the weekend at Two Harbors, made famous as the place where Natalie Wood drowned.

I swam around the boat a few times and was hauled aboard by my companion dripping wet. I had dried everything except my feet before I descended into the cabin and, fortunately, had the presence of mind to hang on while doing so. Regardless, I slipped and cut my knee so badly that I needed immediate attention. Requiring fast medical attention isn't a good thing at Catalina, especially if you're at Two Harbors. Avalon, where there are doctors and a clinic, is a good two to three hours away, whether by land or sea.

We had radioed ahead and were met at the dock by a vehicle that passed as an ambulance and were driven to the only settlement around—a few houses, hotels, bars, and dormitories for workers at the opposite side of the island.

The Angel

While I was trying to figure out the best way to get to Avalon, an angel appeared. "Can I be of any help?" he asked.

It wasn't really an angel, but it was a pediatrician willing to stitch me up. I have forgotten the man's name but will never forget his kindness. Though I offered to pay, he declined, claiming the paperwork would be more trouble than it was worth.

Shortly thereafter I dropped out of the sailing club to pursue more land based activities, like playing bridge and dancing.

My experiences on sailing vessels have not diminished my love for the ocean. I am a Pisces, a water sign and, drawn like a fish to water, Ventura is my natural habitat.

Migrating Monarch Butterflies

More than 185 million Monarch butterflies arrive at sanctuaries in Mexico every year around the end of October, millions of them stopping in the eucalyptus trees in and around Ventura on their way.

Scientists say a good year for butterflies is anytime when there is plenty of moisture to keep their plant food growing and there are few damaging thunderstorms.

The migration is genetic, not learned. The delicate orange-and-black winged creatures who make the journey are the great, great or great, great, great grandchildren of those who made the same migration before. No one is sure how they find their way back.

CHAPTER SEVEN

OTHER PLACES

O ur tour through San Buenaventura has reached the east end of Main Street, but not the end of the adventures. Many remain in other parts of town where spirits cavort and are likely to play jokes on people. One of the most fun sites is a building on Market Street near the Department of Motor Vehicles.

Bikinis Unlimited

Here you will find a suite in an office building that housed a studio specializing in posters and calendars of women clad in bikinis—or less. The space is now rented to a somber group of business persons who wouldn't appreciate having their turf invaded by sightseers should the exact location be identified.

But it is easy to imagine what transpired before. On the second story a doorway is camouflaged as an innocent-looking wall. After pressing a concealed lever, a panel slides back to reveal a cozy apartment. A flight of stairs leads to the rooftop where there is a magnificent view in the distance of the Ventura Marina and Pacific Ocean. There is also enough privacy from prying eyes in surrounding buildings to engage in any type of skullduggery desired.

Crown Books

Before leaving the area, go to the Crown Bookstore at 4756 Telephone Road, B3. Their slogan is, "When it comes to low prices, we wrote the book."

Adult Education

There is something about communities with educational institutions that have a special radiance. You notice it immediately when you arrive in a city where a great school or university is located.

Though Ventura is not fortunate enough to have a university, we do have a terrific junior college that projects the same energy, albeit to a lesser degree. This glow extends to the learning pods around the city like the one described below.

Quilt-making and Wearable Art

After we leave the bookstore we will stay on Telephone Road until we get to the Buenaventura Apartments at 9050 where a treat of another type awaits. Here people are busily engaged in learning how to make quilts and creative clothing described as "wearable art."

Tuesdays from 6:30 to 9:30 p.m. and Wednesdays from 9 a.m. to noon, Jenny Carr-Kinney is the instructor. On Thursdays from 6:30 to 9:30 p.m., Barbara Black presides. Enrollment is ongoing and the class is open to the public.

Their lesson outline gives an overview of the course. "Teach new skills, increase skill levels, encourage free thinking." The day I visited the class it was well attended and all the participants were enjoying themselves.

Quilts have a special appeal for me because they remind me of the warmth and caring involved in the long hours it takes to create one. A hand-sewn wedding ring pattern made by my maternal Grandmother Oldaker is still in the family, gracing the Seattle bedroom of my daughter Vivian and son-in-law Dan.

Trader Joe's

On the way out of town stop in at Trader Joe's at 1751 South Victoria Avenue. This grocery store is so popular it has almost become a legend. You need something unusual? Trader Joe's usually has it, like the green chili salsa to use in a Mexican casserole I was taking to my Spanish Class Christmas party.

Their prices are highly competitive and the selection outstanding. But what has always impressed me is that the people working here seem to genuinely like their jobs. They are so kind and helpful you get the feeling they are having a good time and want you to have a good time, too.

The next stop is one of those places where as soon as you enter you feel welcome.

Somis Market

As long as you are near the 101 and heading out of town anyway, there's no reason to turn back before visiting the Somis Market. Go inland on Victoria until you come to the 126 and veer right to the 118/Los Angeles Avenue. Pass Camarillo and keep going until you arrive at Somis Road.

Since there is only one way to turn you can't miss this tiny town and their locally famous market. It's a long way, but the warmth you feel, the friendly faces you see and the homemade Mexican food they serve make the trip worthwhile.

Papa's

This restaurant reminds me of the movie *Bell, Book and Candle,* starring Jimmy Stewart, Kim Novak and a cat named Pyewacket. Novak was a good witch who lost her powers when she fell in love with a mortal. "Pye," as Novak called her, caught on to her owner's desertion before anyone and became very hostile. This witch isn't nearly as pretty as Kim Novak.

Whether you believe witches and felines are soul mates or any of the other nonsense in the movie, cat lovers will enjoy this place. Nestled in a shopping center at 7822 Telegraph Road, Papa's is an eatery with a cat motif featuring fresh egg custard and other gourmet fare.

Glass Repair
Return to Ventura via the 101 to Johnson Drive and check out the repair shop behind Toys R Us. Though they are expensive, they can repair glass and crystal, sometimes making things look good as new.

If you have broken something but still have usable pieces, The Glass Doctor will do a good job for you, too. He is often found at the swap meets held at the fairgrounds.

Our next destination is a church at the corner of Telegraph Road and Teloma. Before venturing in, let's take a moment to mourn the passing of a colorful event that took place on Teloma. For years the street was ablaze with lights at Christmas time as the residents decorated their homes to celebrate the holidays. Unfortunately, traffic became such a problem the project was abandoned.

The Buenaventura Bridge Club
If you are a bridge enthusiast in search of heart-pounding thrills in a place where you are relatively safe and always welcome, join the fun at the First Christian Church, 38 Teloma Road. Tuesdays and Wednesdays, beginning at 12:30 p.m., bridge players can spend many exciting hours with congenial but highly competitive opponents.

Competition bridge is a challenging sport, ideally suited for those who have backs, necks, legs, or arms that can no longer tolerate the more physical activities they enjoyed before those body parts began wearing out. People like this type of game because, if they are going to do well, they have to keep their brains engaged. Anyone who has found social bridge unchallenging, is welcome to call owner/director Bill Lansing at (805) 642-6284. Need a partner? He'll find one for you.

If you have heard that duplicate players take the game seriously you heard right. I find the game exciting, my blood surging as rapidly through my veins when trying to bring home a Grand Slam as it does when I find a new lover.

Garden Village Café and Mounds Nursery

Right around the corner from the First Christian Church, at 40 North Day Road, is one of the most enchanting gardens in town. The café is unique with its high ceiling and informal atmosphere.

A delightful part of this setting is the area behind it where you can take your food to dine in seclusion or in shady, overgrown alcoves with friends. You may want to wander along the paths where you might suddenly come upon a child-sized house or playground equipment.

Across the street from Ventura College, this café caters to the younger set. Their brochure says, "Live entertainment every weekend. Play ping pong. Surf the 'net.' Check E-mail. Ask us about playing horseshoes and croquet... coming soon to the village."

H. P. Wright Library

This library, at 57 Day Road, did much to take up the slack when the one downtown was being remodeled. Here I continued my pursuit of the offerings of mystery writers and found many written by Erle Stanley Gardner.

Women's libbers would be offended if an author wrote books like this today, so chauvinistic are they. But Gardner didn't mean anything bad by it. When he was alive women were supposed to be subservient to men, work only as secretaries and nurses and, after marrying, stay home and raise their families. I can remember being very comfortable with that philosophy, deciding at an innocent age that when I grew up I was going to get married, have children, and live happily ever after. Life has a way of changing our plans, mine radically—thank God!

Swap Meet and Farmers' Market

Every Saturday and Sunday the college hosts a swap meet. Hundreds of venders rent space to display their wares and services in this always well-attended event. Those who participate regularly need a permit.

Farmer's market has some of the best fresh produce prices in town. Most of the merchants speak English as a second language so shopping here is like a mini visit to Mexico.

Ventura College

This two-year institution has been a beneficial influence in the community ever since it opened, especially for people who cannot afford to live away from home long enough to graduate from a four-year college.

Graphology Classes and Cases

The Community Services Department has been good to me, adding handwriting analysis to the curriculum as soon as I moved to town. These classes are challenging to teach because most of the students have high IQs and are curious to learn something new. Many of them are also interested in the occult sciences, so we are able to connect at a spiritual as well as an intellectual level.

Graphology involves more than identifying personality traits seen in handwriting; it is also used to solve mysteries. Three cases in particular come to mind. The first was a felon, still on parole, who knew if he signed a certain document he would be sent back to prison So he forged *his own signature* in front of his attorney's secretary, a notary public, and got away with it by claiming someone in the lawyer's office had done it. Though my examination proved conclusively the ex-con was the guilty party, the attorney settled out of court to avoid a scandal.

The second case involved an itinerant worker who had been in and out of jails and prisons for decades, accused of endorsing a bogus check. Not only did the poor fellow *not* do it, he *couldn't* have done it. One of the inflexible rules of the science is that you cannot write better than your best.

He was given a choice. He could face a jury of local citizens who were not fond of itinerant workers and take his chances of going back to prison for the rest of his life, or he could confess, spend a few months in jail, then be free to leave town. Considering the bleak alternatives, he confessed to a crime he had not committed.

The third case is one known in the business as a "romantically discovered will." This is always a document discovered after the individual who has allegedly written it is deceased, and it always disinherits the rightful heirs and leaves everything to someone else. The will, holographic (completely handwritten) or just signed by the decedent, is "accidentally" found in such places as under the mattress, in an old book, etc. In the case I am thinking of it was found in a box of papers underneath the dead woman's bed.

Sure enough, allegedly written the day after she had just had one drawn up at her attorney's office, the caregiver got everything. What was interesting about this case was that there was no question the decedent had written it. There was good reason to believe it had been done after she was no longer in control of her faculties.

Unfortunately for the rightful heirs, after years of litigation in which the lawyers, handwriting experts, and others got most of the money, they settled out of court.

Long's Drugstore

At the corner of Ashwood and Telegraph is a business I go out of my way to patronize. Why? I don't know. I think it's because I always feel good when I'm there.

College Care Pharmacy

Next door to Long's is a building with a pharmacy, post office, and gift store. It is filled with a warm energy that makes you want to hang around and browse.

Danny's Deli and Grill

You know the sinking feeling you get when you enter an eating establishment during the lunch hour and find it almost empty? That won't happen here. This deli at 3263 Telegraph Road is always crowded. As Ami and I walked inside we were greeted by two attractive young women. Tantalizing odors wafted toward me, a clue to the quality of the food they serve.

Their menu is varied and the prices are reasonable. They offer appetizers, a wide variety of sandwiches, salads, traditional deli entrees such as hot brisket of beef, and a children's menu. Their wine list, though short, is reasonably priced, so while you're in town, try Danny's.

Big Yellow House

Ami and I leave Ventura now, heading northwest on the 101 Freeway to Summerland and a business near the ocean we missed before while searching for the nude beach. The Big Yellow House is a historic home that has been turned into a restaurant. And it is haunted.

"Is Hector still around?" I asked the waitress.

"Oh yes. Just a couple of weeks ago one of our cooks saw him in the kitchen."

He was first spotted by Rod Lathim a quarter of a century ago when Lathim was managing the Wine Cellar and Gift Shop. "As I worked I became increasingly aware of an invisible presence. I regularly heard footsteps when there was no one around but me.

It was a playful spirit, full of mischief, and unpredictable. I figured out it was a young boy and for no particular reason, named him Hector."

Unlike the owners of Landmark No. 78 who promote their ghost, Rosa, the owner of the Big Yellow House downplays stories about Hector. "I guess he thinks it would turn customers away," Lathim said, "but it might do just the opposite."

Swing back toward Ventura, leave the 101, and drive north on the 33 Freeway. Glimpses of Lake Casitas to the west are occasionally visible en route to Oakview and Ojai. The latter is a little burg full of psychic energy, terrific eateries, musicians, artists, and movie stars who have fled the City of Angels hoping to find respite from the hectic Hollywood scene.

Before Ami and I get to Ojai we have a few stops to make.

Nye Mansion

Alongside the River Trail on the 33, we turn off at Casitas Vista Road and are soon in Foster Park. This area is always cool, even in the hottest days of summer. Some people speculate it's because it's so close to a haunted house.

We don't linger but quickly pass over the bridge and turn onto Santa Ana Road where the Nye Mansion is located.

Once painted pink, with a forlorn For Sale sign in front of it for a number of years, it is now white and looks like it is occupied. A German shepherd who has been lying on the front porch rises and wags his tail in friendly greeting as my car comes to a halt. A swing hangs from a big shade tree in the front yard. I don't attempt to go inside because the residents are not expecting me—and because of stories I've heard.

Legend has it that the place was inhabited by members of the Nye family for generations. One of the women was bludgeoned to death in a domestic violence dispute. As the descendants grew older and gradually died off, the place stood empty, difficult to sell because of its bloody history. This information was gleaned from newspaper stories and other articles found at the mission library, and from myths and legends surrounding the mansion that have been circulating in Ventura a long time. It is a part of our mystique, characteristic of spirits and stories that cling to old cities.

Center for Earth Concerns

Back on the 33 we proceed to 150 Baldwin Road where the Center for Earth Concerns is located. Their brochure says:

Love Mother Nature. Learn and work for nature.

Welcome! The Center for Earth Concerns is based in the Ojai Valley and consists of 275 acres of woodlands, meadows, chaparral, and year-round streams. It is home to one of Southern California's finest botanical gardens.

The Center is nestled at the headwaters of Lake Casitas surrounded by the Los Padres National Forest.

Our Mission: To be a major resource for individual and community organizations that want to learn about and contribute to the protection of nature and the environment.

Their projects include a parrot sanctuary, botanical garden, environmental education, and a floating classroom on Lake Casitas.

You can get involved by becoming a docent, volunteering as a gardener, adopting a rescued bird, or building an aviary. If you are genuinely concerned about these issues you will want to contact them. You can also help out by holding your special events here. Looking for an innovative location for a wedding or social gathering? If so, this Mediterranean setting is a gracious, creative choice.

The Iron Monster

As the 20th Century began Nordhoffians were planning a big party to celebrate the completion of the rail line into what is now Ojai. But not everyone was happy about it. Some considered the iron horse to be a monster invading the seclusion of their peaceful valley. Shortly after the first steam engine huffed into the city, the editor of the local newspaper, the Ojai News, received this letter, undoubtedly written by a child with an overactive imagination.

Dear Editor,

Now that the railroad has arrived in Nordhoff I wish you would describe the engine for the information of my neighbors and myself who have never seen one. Does it look anything like an elephant?

My brother, Bobby, and I want to go to Nordhoff to see it, but Ma is afraid we might never come back home alive. Is it really dangerous?

And would it be safe for us to stand close enough to get a good to look at it?

Respectfully...

After a series of devastating floods Mother Nature dealt a final blow to the railroad which had done so much for the valley and the two cities it linked. In 1969 the valley received 40 inches of rain in a two-week period. The railroad became the target of the deluge and the tracks were washed out for the final time. In 1980 the County of Ventura acquired the land from the Southern Pacific and built a horse and bike trail on the narrow stretch, the forerunner of what has become The River Trail.

Amelda's Guest Ranch

Many businesses along the Ojai Valley route attribute their success to the arrival of the Iron Horse. One in particular was the well-known, Amelda's Guest Ranch. Set on a city-sized lot, it enjoyed a spectacular view.

The imposing "ranch house" was a multi-storied Georgian with a green mansard roof. A verandah wrapped around three sides. The windows were tall and slender and covered with velvet draperies that were tied with gold cord. The lovely ladies that acted as hostesses added the final touch of class.

In the lower level of the building there were small "offices" for the use of the "hostesses." They had no windows or typewriters but there didn't seem to be many complaints. The ladies were paid well and enjoyed their work.

When business was slow Amelda would advertise in the Ojai News and point out that she did indeed have *reasonable rates.*

Tragedy not only hit the railroad during this time, but Amelda's as well. One of the hostesses, while working to increase her household budget, was caught by a very jealous husband who shot both his wife and the gentleman who was kind enough to be helping the woman increase her earnings. Amelda was forced to close her guest ranch because of the scandal.

Today the building is owned by the Ojai Valley Racquet Club. A banner across the front says, *"Southern California's Full-time Boarding Academy and Prep School."*

Haunting Visitors

On our way back to Ventura we travel along the scenic 150 Freeway to the 126 Freeway and then get on the 118/Los Angeles Avenue exit where last December a death occurred. According to Jeannine, the woman who told me about it, her female roommate was driving to Ventura with her daughter, missed a curve and lost control of the car when it hit the shoulder. The mother threw herself across her little girl to protect her from the ensuing crash. The mother died; the 12-year-old survived.

Afterward, Jeannine kept seeing the dead woman's ghost in her doorway. She was not a threatening presence, just stood there gazing at her. Jeannine called me when she heard I was writing a book that had ghost stories in it and asked why her former roommate kept coming back.

"I don't know," I replied. "Is she worried about her daughter?"

"Probably, since she has to live with her father and his girl-friend, who hates her."

I referred the woman to Richard Senate. He knows a lot more about ghosts than I do. Some psychic individuals can occasionally predict events.

Betty G. once told me, "A few years I was wakened by a loud voice in my bedroom which I recognized as belonging to my former mother-in-law. She was saying, 'Betty, I want you to know I love you.' I told her I loved her, too, then called my former husband. I knew his mother had been very ill and thought she might have died. A week later, at the same time, she passed away.

"On the bus going to work one night I saw a man sitting on one of the seats, bent over, as if in great pain. I recognized him as a friend named Leon. A week later, to my surprise, Leon's wife, Deb, called and told me Leon had passed away quite unexpectedly at age 46. He'd had a heart attack, the result of a birth defect no one had ever suspected."

Computer Ghosts

This book is full of stories about ghosts and other unexplained energies. Some of them reside in my computer. This phenomenon has been explained as a "screen saver," but it looks like spirits to me. Whenever I stop using the mouse or keyboard for any length of time, even to print something, a strange picture appears.

It depicts a two-story house plus an attic, painted white with gray trim. The sky is dark, a full moon hangs overhead and a wise old owl perched on the branch of a dead tree stares at me unblinkingly. Weird things happen. There is a light on in a downstairs room. It goes off and another goes on upstairs, then in the attic. As a bat flutters past, the front door opens but no one goes in or out.

After the door closes, the light goes off upstairs and shortly thereafter the entire house is dark. This seems to occur without benefit of human occupancy. So the computer sympathizes with the apparitions that haunt San Buenaventura. What fascinates me is how the computer, or the people who sold it to me, knew I was going to be writing such a book before I knew it myself. Whatever the reason, I feel the spirit world nearby.

Fax Machine Fairy

How could I possibly begin getting faxes intended for Patagonia on my machine unless the thing was haunted? Yet that is exactly what happened.

Thinking it was a onetime occurrence I notified the sender, then sent a copy to Patagonia and asked them to tell their subsidiaries not to send faxes to me. To no avail. They kept arriving; I kept calling them. They didn't return the calls.

More faxes, more explanations of what was happening left with their receptionist. Finally, a response on my answering machine said, "I don't understand the message."

And then one morning at 3:00 a.m. I received a 12-page inventory list from one of their outlets in Australia. That did it! My fax is noisy and two feet from the head of my bed. I was so frustrated I started throwing the stuff away, figuring surely someday someone would catch on to what was happening and put a stop to it.

Months later someone who worked at Patagonia called and asked if I was getting any of their messages.

"Quite a few."

"Would you please forward them to us?"

When I patiently explained I had done that over and over again, they were nonplussed, unable to understand what caused the mix-up since their numbers are so different from mine.

I can explain it easily. It's because something was going on "up there."

This fiasco was nothing compared to the time some goblins caused an incorrect listing to get into the Yellow Pages.

Escort Service Imp

The phone rang at 2 a.m. Afraid something had happened to one of the children I answered it.

"Hi! Can you shend a girl to my hotel room?"

"WHAT?"

"A girl. You know, one of those danshers."

"What are you talking about?" Stupid drunk.

"Isn't this.....?" He named a local escort service.

I couldn't believe it. The directory had printed a single digit mistake. My phone became an escort service's, and there was nothing the yellow pages personnel could do about it until the new directory was published.

Though logically I know who was responsible for the error, intuitively I believe things happen with my machines that can't be explained so simply. One of the sprites I sometimes see playing in the garden on dark, misty nights had either lost its way or had come into the apartment on purpose, just to let me know it was around. For a year I had to disconnect the phone before I went to bed to keep the imp from interrupting my sleep.

The Answering Machine Angst

It must be a diabolical plot, all the things that goof up the mechanical things in my place. Why else would the answering machine capriciously chop off some messages mid-sentence and let others play as long as they like? The gremlins in there cause me great angst, always deciding, just before the caller gives critical information, to play dirty tricks and cut off the most important part. I am going to foil it by asking everyone to leave their phone number first, and see if this ploy can keep this kind of nonsense from happening in the future.

Printer Pranks

The printer is as mischievous as everything else around my habitat. Smeared words and strange symbols occasionally spew forth from this "time-saving" device. Once Don, my computer guru, saw what was happening (timing was off) and fixed it, the printer began behaving better.

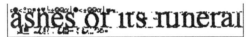

The Hot Spot

After reading about Feng Shui I discovered why I burn things in my kitchen all the time. It's because you can see the stove from the entrance. According to the book, that is very bad chi. What can I do about it? I can't change the entrance or keep the kitchen door closed because it's a pair of filigreed wooden screens. I will probably have to keep eating burnt garlic bread. I'm certainly used to it.

These culinary sacrifices began in my childhood when Mother would cook t-bone steaks in the oven under the broiler—one steak to be divided amongst the six of us. She always shut the oven door to "keep the heat in," unmindful of the smoke pouring out that got so thick we children had to go out onto the back porch in order to breathe.

Now, whenever I burn food, I am reminded of an old saying, "The fruit does not fall far from the tree."

My stove isn't the only appliance that plays tricks on people. Consider what happened to the hapless woman who was helping a friend give a party for 20 luncheon guests. She couldn't get the hors d'oeuvres baked. Not used to an electric stove, every time she shut the oven door she also closed the latch.

You're not supposed to do this until you clean it because if you do, the heat won't come on.

A stove in an apartment in a hangar at the airport in Santa Paula gave Jack, its owner, a worse scare.

Arriving home one afternoon Jack found his cat huddled in a corner. Entering the kitchen, he discovered why. Earlier he had been boiling eggs and had forgotten to turn off the stove before he left. After the water boiled away the eggs blew up all over the walls and ceiling, frightening his pet out of some of her nine lives.

The Phoenix Flight

The hangar at 848 E. Santa Maria Street is home base for an innovative business—aerial scattering of loved ones' remains.

The owners, Margaret "Maggie" Bird and Glenn C. True, Jr., are fully certified pilots with thousands of flight hours logged and more than 25 years' experience.

"Some of the things that happen are heartwarming enough to bring tears to your eyes," Maggie said. "Recently, after we had dropped rose petals over those gathered on the beach in Ventura to watch the ceremony, and had scattered the ashes, one of the deceased woman's sons swam out to where the remains had been strewn to place a wreath on the watery grave. On the way back to shore he was accompanied by three dolphins."

Poinsettia Dance Club

Now that our adventures have circled back to Ventura, don't miss the dance held every Monday night at the Poinsettia Center, 3451 Foothill Road. Live ballroom music, great facilities and a spectacular view of the Pacific shoreline make these dances some of happiest social events in the city. They start at 8:00 and end at 10:30 with a break in the middle for refreshments. For more information call the Pavilion at 648-1143.

The Long Dark Limousine

It was New Year's Eve and I was returning home from a party as gala as a Hollywood premiere. As the marine layer rolled in I witnessed a sad and haunting sight. While waiting at a traffic signal, a very long, very dark limousine drove aimlessly across the intersection before me. A young male voice shouted "Happy New Year!" and one firecracker was thrown from a rear window.

Disturbed by the lonely feeling surrounding this scene, I speculated about the occupant. Why had he no one to celebrate with? What was his story? Did he welcome the comforting presence of the fog, or did he find it threatening?

After the light changed to green, beckoning me toward my cozy home, I realized many individuals' futures are not bright. They're all not people who are homeless or poor either. Some of them can afford to drive around in luxurious vehicles.

As the limousine slowly disappeared from view, a mist shrouded the city and, in the distance, a foghorn warned of treacherous, rock-strewn shoals. It would be this way all night.

Amazons

Centuries ago during the dark ages, a tale was spun by a storyteller named Montalvo about a mythical woman called Queen Califa who ruled over the kingdom of California. It was a land of milk and honey where fruit and flowers grew wild and life was a paradise on earth. This magical place was inhabited by Amazons, gorgeous women who ate their mates after they had served their purpose.

Juan Rodriguez Cabrillo, a Portuguese explorer sailing under the flag of Spain, is the one who named this area. Expecting to find rich cities and a passageway between the Atlantic and Pacific Oceans, Cabrillo was so disappointed in the barrenness of the land he named it "California" as a joke. According to a 1963 edition of *The World Book Encyclopedia* and a current Web site definition, California is named after a treasure island paradise described in a Spanish tale of the early 1500s.

How amazed Cabrillo and his fellow explorers would be to return today, for Ventura is as close to paradise as any place on earth can be. Flowers decorate the landscape the year around, crops flourish in the fields, fruit weighs down the branches of trees. And the women are breathtaking. Though they no longer reign supreme, or eat their mates very often, the leggy beauties inhabiting our streets and beaches are lovely enough and tall enough and intelligent enough to be the Amazons of our ancestors' fantasies.

Epilogue

Outer Spaces

Two of my favorite places on Planet Earth are so far from Ventura they have no business being in this book. Since I have always enjoyed them so much, and believe you will too, I offer them as afterthoughts.

Highway One

We leave Ventura heading for a couple of places that are great fun and definitely worth seeing. The first is Venice/Muscle Beach, the second most popular (after Disneyland) tourist site in California.

We get there by driving along the spectacularly scenic Coast Highway. As we journey southward we pass beaches where, on weekends, hordes of tanned people surf and swim and enjoy the sun, sand, and year-round warm weather. We catch glimpses of the romantic city of Malibu and spectacularly beautiful Pepperdine University Campus. Soon after we get to Venice we reach our first destination.

Venice's Muscle Beach

Like beaches everywhere, the one at Venice is filled with a mystic force that rolls in off the water. To describe it as spiritual is incorrect, for there is too much mixed chi surging around.

It is like hearing a pianist hit a wrong key, or a tenor's voice cracking on a high note. Duos of sturdy male police officers patrolling the area are a reminder this is Los Angeles. The entire area occasionally has to be closed when troublemakers become too rowdy.

Though this undercurrent of danger makes the visit more of an adventure, nothing traumatic ever happened when I've been there. So let me tell you what did occur.

This seaside resort is often called Muscle Beach because of the hunks running around in various stages of nudity. Not to be outdone are Playboy Bunny beautiful young women similarly attired.

I met one of the latter recently. She is petite and curvaceous and has long red hair. Weekdays she works for a talent agency. Weekends she spends with her boyfriend who moonlights as a puppeteer. On Saturdays and Sundays they hang out at the beach where he gives free shows and sells puppets and she searches for people who might become tomorrow's hottest movie stars.

There is a man who attracts crowds juggling chain saws while they are turned on, and a row of psychics offering Tarot, Palm, Numerology, and Astrology readings. There was a reflexologist who poked the bottom of my big toe with her fingernail and, when I jerked my foot away, told me I needed to drink more water. Dutifully I began drinking THREE quarts a day and continued until I visited the same woman a year later.

Not recognizing me, she poked the bottom of my big toe with her thumbnail again and, when I jerked my foot away, said the same thing. What I told her was along the lines of intense disbelief in her healing psychic abilities.

The activities of this cross-section of the human race would be difficult to find anywhere else. You may witness technicians filming scenes from movies like *White Men Can't Jump* or athletes whose faces you recognize playing basketball. You might stumble across film legends, or innocents who want to be.

During one visit Ami commented on the number of prosperous looking, middle-aged men we saw walking aimlessly back and forth.

"What are they doing?" she asked. "It's Sunday. They should be at home with their families or at a movie or something. They're obviously not vagrants, so what's going on?"

They are trolling. Once in a while you see a guy who has landed a real prize, a suntanned beauty less than half his age who has a great body.

How these aging geezers with middle-aged spreads are able to accomplish this is not difficult to understand. Many aspiring actors fall for a line from someone who claims he is an agent or a producer who can help them with their careers—for a few considerations. It's the modern day version of the casting couch.

Others, usually men, have the wherewithal to help a struggling young woman or teenager far from home by setting her up in a modest apartment nowhere near his wife or family but close enough for his convenience.

The things you see here stagger the imagination. No wonder it's so popular.

Our next stop can only be reached by going overseas to London, England, a favorite destination for thousands of Americans every year.

Whenever I asked friends who had visited the United Kingdom about what I should do when I was there I was always referred to popular tourist meccas like museums, theaters, malls, and parks.

That wasn't what I was searching for. I would rather discover a basement in an out-of-the-way hotel in Knightsbridge where I could enjoy a game of duplicate bridge. How about connecting me with a person who has lived in Great Britain all his or her life who knows where to find places not listed in tourist brochures? I pick the brains of people like my son-in-law Les who was born and raised there and is a Brit through and through (though not too English to marry an American woman).

My other favorite nook, which is in London, is described below.

Books for Cooks

JoAnn found out about this place when she had a flat in London and became acquainted with many of the natives. Located at 4 Blenheim Crescent, it sells cookbooks from shelves stacked to the ceiling. As fun as it is to browse through them, it is even more delightful to have lunch.

Many of the books are written by gourmet chefs who come in periodically to prepare their specialties. Though the restaurant part is small and usually crowded, it is worth the inconvenience to watch the way the authors, many of whom are young women, prepare and serve the luscious food.

You can reach them by calling 011 44 020 7221 1922 or faxing them at 011 44 020 7221 1517. Reservations are mandatory.

Notting Hill

After you leave Books for Cooks nip around the corner to the apartment with the blue door where the movie *Notting Hill* was filmed. Though I understand the door is no longer blue, any merchant in the area can direct you to it.

Haunted Castle

"My children and I were sightseeing," Ami said. "I don't remember exactly where the castle was located, but I do remember the name started with a B.

"I had become separated from the others and wandered upstairs onto a balcony. As I stood enjoying the view I became aware of a presence behind me. Turning, I saw an apparition dressed in white that had no hands, head, or feet. Though the air around me was still, the garments it wore billowed toward me. Frightened, I hurried away to rejoin my loved ones."

This sighting took place in Merry Olde England.

Our journey has come to an end. I hope you have enjoyed these mystical escapades as much as I have enjoyed sharing them with you.

INDEX